This book is dedicated to my children,
Jacob, Becca and A. J.
You are my inspiration. Although I can't
protect you from the chaos of the world,
I hope you will always find stability in the
knowledge that I love you unconditionally.
No parent has a greater reason
to celebrate his children than I.

And to my wife, who is the true rock of the family.
I'm not sure I could do it without you;
I wouldn't even want to try!

CONTENTS

ACKNOWLEDGMENTS

"Writing is easy. All you do is stare at a blank sheet of paper until drops of blood form on your forehead," wrote Gene Fowler. I know the feeling. I have often likened writing a book to having a baby. After a lot of forethought (literary foreplay!), you finally conceive an idea, develop it for nine to twelve months, endure the painful process of delivering a final manuscript, then immediately forget about the pain while you bask in the glow of your beautiful "baby."

And like having a baby, a person cannot give birth to a book by himself. Behind every author stands a veritable army of people without whose support, advice and assistance, a good idea would remain just that. I am particularly lucky to have had the help of some outstanding people.

Drs. David Elkind, John Friel, Sal Severe, Marilyn Sorenson, Margot Maine, Jim Loomis, Peter Czuczka, John Bruer, Maureen Weiss, John DiFiori, Steve Baskin, Randy Weeks and Lynne Drabkin were kind enough to share their expertise with me. I can't thank them enough for their help.

Thank you also to Aileen Dickey, whom I have known for many years. I am glad our paths have crossed once again.

There were many people who were generous enough to share with me stories about themselves, or about their friends and family members. In most cases, I have changed their names in order to protect their privacy. However, I owe them a huge debt of gratitude; they know who they are. Other people, such as Jim Gondek, David Cooley, Chet Speiser, Nancy Femiano, Davis Glasser, Ali Murdoch and Louveda Morris, allowed me to use their real names, so I am happy to be able to recognize their contributions publicly.

Thank you to Jane Hansen, Robi Ludwig and again to Drs. Friel and Severe for their generous comments about the book. It was an honor to have each of them review the manuscript prior to its publication.

I would be remiss if I didn't thank all my wonderful NBC colleagues for supporting me during the research, writing and promotion of this book. At WVIT (NBC 30), my old stomping grounds in Hartford: Liz Grey, Gerry Brooks, Joanne Nesti, Janet Peckinpaugh and the rest of the gang. At WNBC in New York: Dianne Doctor, Joel Goldberg, Shelly Harper, Nancy Han, Jaimee Silverstein, Karen Harris, Jane Hansen, Maurice Dubois and everyone else involved in producing *Today in New York*.

Since this book is about parenting, it would be strange if I didn't acknowledge my own parents, Stuart and Mimi Marks. They created the environment in which I was able to flourish and strive to reach my potential. I always knew that they were there for me. They still are. So are my other parents, my in-laws, Ralph and Lynne Drabkin. From day one, they have treated me as their son. I am lucky to have not one, but two sets of incredibly generous and supportive parents.

A lot of the stories in this book are based on patients that I, or another physician, took care of at the New England Center for Headache. The name of every patient has been changed in order to maintain patient confidentiality. I must thank them nonetheless. It was an honor being their physician. Thank you also to the co-founders of the New England Center for Headache, Drs. Alan Rapoport and Fred Sheftell.

This book would never, and I mean never, have come to pass without the support, vision and advice of the people at Health Communications, Inc. My editor, Allison Janse, has believed in this book from the very beginning and I can't thank her enough for her help in molding the manuscript until it took on just the right shape. Sometimes I wanted to tear my hair out at the thought of having to do more work on what I thought was a "completed" manuscript, but invariably Allison's advice was right on the money.

Randee Feldman, Kim Weiss, Christine Belleris, Maria Dinoia, Tom Sand, Lawna Patterson Oldfield, Dawn Grove, Bob Land, Peter Vegso, and the rest of the staff at HCI were also instrumental in helping me birth this book.

Then there's Julie Eckhert, my agent and close friend, who believes in me so much that she is able to promote me better than I could ever promote myself. Without her there would be no books, no newspaper articles, no television career. She knows more about the media than anyone I know and she teaches me something new virtually every day. And

I appreciate her continuing efforts to help me reach my professional potential. You can detect her fingerprints on everything I do in my career.

Finally, and most importantly, there's my family, from whom I draw my inspiration and without whom none of this would be worthwhile. My wife, Laura, has always been my biggest supporter. She has an uncanny ability to prop me up when I'm in a rut and to cheer me on when I'm on a roll. She is also the best physician I have ever known; it's no surprise that patients flock to her. Her experience as a pediatrician was invaluable to me while writing this book. Almost as invaluable is her patience and understanding of this sometimes bizarre career path I have chosen. When we married, she undoubtedly thought she was settling down with a doctor who would join a practice, have steady hours, and lead a fairly normal and predictable life. Boy was she wrong! Yet she has stuck by me through thick and thin. She is truly my soul mate.

I am also blessed with three wonderful kids, Jacob, Becca and A. J. They are the most important things in my life. I try to practice what I preach in this book, but if at times I falter, I hope they will always know how much I love them.

PART I

The World
Around Us

ONE

A NEW WORLD
DISORDER

As for most American families, September 11, 2001, started out like any other Tuesday in the Marks household. I did my normal health report on the morning news show at WNBC-TV in New York City and left Rockefeller Center at approximately 7:30 A.M. When I arrived home an hour later, my wife had already left for work and my two oldest kids were on their way to school. I decided to take a nap.

Forty-five minutes after I fell asleep, our baby-sitter woke me. She was crying, but she managed to tell me to turn on the television. I watched in horror as the television showed, over and over again, the pictures of the airplane attacks on the World Trade Center Towers and their subsequent collapse.

As a parent, my job in a crisis is to make certain the family is safe; as a reporter, my job in a crisis is to go where the story is. The competing pressures tore at me. I thought I came up with a reasonable compromise: I rushed to Bridgeport Hospital, in Bridgeport, Connecticut—one of the trauma and burn centers where survivors were expected to be taken. Bridgeport is only a few miles from my house, and going there offered an ideal solution to my dilemma. I could report on the tragedy and still stay close to home and make sure my family was safe. By late evening, however, everyone knew that the number of survivors would be few indeed.

When I returned home for dinner after the evening news, my wife Laura and I decided we would try to shield our children from the World Trade Center disaster. Jacob, six, and Becca, four, had already seen pictures of one of the plane crashes. Our babysitter had been glued, nearly apoplectically, to the television all day and had inadvertently let the kids see the dreadful footage. We told them a plane had accidentally flown into the building, which seemed to suffice. (We didn't have to worry about our youngest son, A. J., because he was only a year old.) We ate, talked about school, played a board game, read books and put the kids to sleep as usual. Then I left for New York City.

I worked virtually around the clock for the first week after the disaster. I occasionally went to my in-laws' Manhattan apartment to catch a few hours of sleep and a hot meal, but I spent most of my time at Bellevue Hospital in lower Manhattan, at Ground Zero or in the WNBC studios at Rockefeller Center. I spoke to my family on the phone, but I didn't see them for almost an entire week.

When I returned home, Laura pulled me aside and whispered, "I think Jacob's really stressed out right now."

"Why do you say that?" I asked.

"He's blinking a lot," she answered. "I've tried to talk to him about it, but he says nothing's bothering him. He won't talk about it at all, but he keeps blinking. Go see for yourself."

Laura was right. During previous periods of intense stress, Jacob experienced episodes of blinking. He spoke and acted normally, but every few seconds his eyes blinked, like an eye twitch. He didn't know he was doing it, or at least he never said anything about it. Every other time, Jacob stopped blinking as soon as the stress receded.

We thought of a few likely reasons for Jacob's anxiety. September was a stressful month for us even before the events of the eleventh. We had bought a house the week before, and the children were beginning to deal with the thought of packing up all of their belongings and moving from the only house they had ever known. We knew this process would be especially hard on Jacob. He had just started first grade, made a new group of friends, and become comfortable with his teacher, class and school. He would now have to change schools and be the new kid in class. He was scheduled to start school in two weeks—even before we moved into the new house.

Jacob tried to put on a brave face about the changes. He told us, "Don't worry, Mommy and Daddy, I'll make new friends." Other statements betrayed his anxiety: "What if I can't find my classroom?" and "They've all made friends with each other," and "What if I'm the only one in my class wearing glasses? Maybe they'll make fun of me." As it turned out, three out of the eighteen kids in his new class wore glasses—much to Jacob's relief.

We talked about the possibility that the terrorist attacks might also have affected Jacob, but we thought this was much less likely a cause than the major life changes closer to home. Besides, as far as we knew, Jacob and Becca thought the crashes were accidental. We wanted to protect them from the truth by not discussing the situation around them and keeping the television off while they were awake. How do you explain to a six-year-old and a four-year-old that people in the world hate them and want to kill them? How can young children be expected to understand that which even most adults are unable to comprehend?

At the dinner table that night, we talked about the new house, about how each of them would have their own room, about what we wanted to do with the backyard and about how great Jacob's new school was supposed to be. Then we played a board game, read books and put the children to bed. We had come up with a strategy to decrease Jacob's anxiety: get him excited about moving and stick to our usual routines as much as possible.

This strategy seemed reasonable, except for one problem. Our plan missed the real source of Jacob's anxiety. This became evident the next day when we were out to lunch with Jacob's grandparents. While we were waiting for our food, the kids were drawing with crayons on the back of their paper place mats. When Jacob finished, he raised his picture and said, "Look at my drawing."

"What is that?" I asked after a moment's hesitation.

"This is an airplane, and these two lines are the Twin Towers. See," he pointed from one to the other, "the airplane is flying into the towers."

The adults around the table looked at each other with raised eyebrows. Then I turned back to the picture and noticed blue crisscrossing lines at the top of the page. I asked what they were.

"That's a jail in the sky for the bad guys to go to in heaven," Jacob said.

We knew he had seen the video of the plane crashes. We were stunned that he knew "bad guys" were involved. Despite our efforts to shelter him from the outside world, the hard, ugly truth seeped through our defenses.

We tried to talk to Jacob about his picture, to reassure him about the situation, but he refused to cooperate and quickly changed the subject. Not until later that night did we realize just how anxious the World Trade Center attacks were making him feel. We were standing in the kitchen when Jacob laughingly commented about "buildings falling down" in Manhattan. When asked again if the events bothered him, he finally began to talk.

"How come Daddy is going back to Manhattan tomorrow? That's where the buildings are falling down and people are getting hurt," he said, the smile now gone from his face.

We explained to him that I had to go because that was my job and I was trying to help people so they wouldn't get hurt. We told him that Manhattan was very safe, that nothing like this had ever happened before, and that the president was going to find the bad guys and punish them. We also reassured him that his grandparents, who live in Manhattan and whose apartment the kids had slept in often, were completely safe and were a long way from where the towers had collapsed. He asked a few more questions, and our answers seemed to allay his fears.

The next day, Jacob woke up and his nervous blinking had stopped. We figured that was the end of the story. We continued to keep him and the other kids away from the television as much as possible, and we maintained the ban on television news while the children were awake. We did not exactly declare victory and light up Cuban cigars, but we certainly felt that we had eased Jacob's anxiety.

A week later, however, we realized just how deeply embedded in his psyche the World Trade Center attacks had become. His first-grade teacher asked the students to draw a picture of their choice. Most kids made a drawing of their family, house, toys, etc. Jacob created a huge, detailed and colorful picture of the Empire State Building with a flaming airplane flying right into it. He said he didn't know why he chose to draw that particular picture; it was just what he "thought of." He made no references to anyone's safety or to the terrorist attacks, nor did his blinking return. Yet his drawing was a sign that, in all likelihood, some small corner of his mind will never again perceive the world as completely safe.

In retrospect, we should have recognized earlier the source of our son's stress. Only when he expressed himself through his drawing did his psychological turmoil become evident. Laura is a pediatrician, and I was in the middle of writing this book about children and stress. If we could misinterpret what was happening with our own son, any parents could do the same with their own children.

The events of September 11 have rocked our world. We thought we were personally safe and insulated from international affairs. We now know better. Most people I know say their lives will never be the same again, and many of them are concerned about raising their children in a dangerous world. They worry about their kids' safety and the prospects for their future, and the possibility that their children will grow up in a constant state of siege, fighting a war without end, with the possibility they will have to deal with an enemy unafraid to use weapons of mass destruction.

These fears are based on reality. We *have* been attacked. We *are* at war with an unseen enemy, one who moves freely among us and could even be living next door. One potential weapon of mass destruction, anthrax, has already been used against us—however crude the delivery method—and there remains the awful possibility that the anthrax attacks came from a disgruntled American. Other, more fearsome weapons also threaten us: smallpox, botulism toxin, nerve gas, nuclear bombs.

The events of September 11 plunged us into a world for which most of us are unprepared. They have created new stresses that claimed new victims: our children. They feel the insecurity and danger, too. Their instinctive, subconscious, intuitive reaction comes from sensing the anxiety and tension in the adults around them.

Jacob is not the only child to express his fears through pictures. Two of our best friends' young children also spontaneously drew their own interpretations of the World Trade Center attacks, and the University of Hartford staged an entire exhibit of similar drawings from other children. Aaron Howard once wrote, "Art is . . . a question mark in the minds of those who want to know what's happening." Imagine the questions our children must now have about the world around them.

One twelve-year-old boy in Florida expressed his concerns well in a poem he wrote:

I wonder if World War Three will break out
I hear planes crashing.
I want these terrorists to show themselves . . .
I pretend to be brave . . .
I try to stay calm.
I hope I don't die.
I am Calm![1]

Other children express themselves less poetically, but just as powerfully. Check out the kids' chat rooms on the Internet to glimpse the impact of September 11:

"On Tuesday, when the attacks on America happened, I was not only scared but also angry with what had happened. This was supposed to be a safe place to live. I feel very upset, and don't know why this had to happen," writes Allison, a girl from Oklahoma.

Another girl named Allyson, this one a twelve-year-old from Arizona, notes, ". . . I am also scared to go to bed now. Every time I hear or see a plane I get scared."[2]

Twelve-year-old Sommer from New York feels the same way: "This has been a fearful and stressful week for me. This was too surprising and random. . . . I do not feel safe even being in my house because this could've happened to anyone at anytime."

The Israelis have a name for this. "We call it the triple-A rule: Anywhere. Anytime. To anyone," says Mooli Lahad, founder of the Community Stress Prevention Center at Telhi College in Kiryat Shmona, a northern Israeli town that Palestinian terrorists frequently target for attack.[3]

The Israelis have had more than fifty years to learn to deal with the triple-A rule. We have barely begun to see its consequences. Citizens of Israel have adjusted their lives to the constant threat of terror; we are still assimilating the meaning of September 11, 2001. Their children learn very early on that they live in a dangerous world; our kids have, until recently, grown up relatively sheltered from those cruel realities. Parents will have many new issues to address in the coming years. If we are indeed at war, then we should be mindful that one-tenth to one-half of war casualties are psycho-logical.[4] Usually, these casualties are soldiers on the front lines. In this war, though, we are all soldiers, and our front yards could very well be the front lines. On this battlefield, the casualties will undoubt-edly include children.

Casualties

"My belly hurts," said Cindy, a four-year-old from New Jersey.

Her mom turned to the pediatrician and added, "She's also had diarrhea every few days or so, and she's been wetting the bed."

"How long has she had the symptoms?" the doctor asked.

"I think it's been about a month now," the mom answered.

The doctor visit took place in the middle of October, a little more than a month after the World Trade Center attacks.

Her story came to me as an example of a child who experienced physical effects from the insecurity and anxiety in the chaos around her. Cindy's mom did not link the terrorist attacks and her daughter's symp-toms, and at four years old, Cindy was unable to ver-balize her anxiety.

Ten-year-old William was able to talk about his fears, but like most ten-year-olds, he didn't. Instead, within weeks of the terrorist attacks, William developed an itchy, scaly rash on the back of his knees and on both of his forearms. The itching was so bad that it kept him up at night. The more he scratched, the more his skin itched.

William had suffered from eczema when he was younger, but the rash had not appeared in the previous two years. Because of the timing of this outbreak, his parents suspected a tie to the World Trade Center attacks. They tried to talk to him about the attacks and about any concerns he might have, but William was tight-lipped and denied any worries.

The doctor agreed that William's eczema was probably anxiety related. In addition to treating the rash with prescription ointments, he encouraged William's parents to continue to talk to their son about the attacks and to reassure him, through their words and actions, that he is safe.

At the time of this writing, William, Cindy and their parents are still struggling with the consequences of the new world disorder. So are thousands of other families across the country, including my own. Jacob is no longer blinking, but he still occasionally draws morbid pictures. Becca woke up with terrible nightmares almost every night the first couple of weeks after September 11; the terrors have now decreased in frequency, but every once in a while she'll still wake up crying from a bad dream.

Children react differently to a disaster, depending upon their distance from it, their age, previous experience with disasters, emotional maturity, temperament and personality. However, disasters cause common feelings in almost all children and adults.[5] They make us feel as though we're not in control of our lives. Indeed, disasters are, by their very nature, out of our control. They make our world seem unstable because they throw off our routines and destroy our sense of trust. They make us feel unsafe.

Terrorism is about making people afraid: afraid to fly, to go to work, to live a normal life. If you want to know how much our lives have changed since September 11, just look at the signs of fear pervading our society. Adults have become so scared to fly that some entertainers wouldn't even attend the Emmy Awards ceremony because they would have had to take a cross-country flight; some people now wear gloves to open their mail; some New Yorkers are moving out of the city; the National Guard patrols our airports; twenty-four-hour cable news channels fill their airtime with talk about the possibility that terrorists have suitcase-sized nuclear bombs. Other adults are less frightened about their safety than they are about whether they will still have jobs tomorrow.

Terrorism scares kids, too. Young children, including those in elementary or middle school, may worry that Mom or Dad is going to be taken away from them or that tall buildings aren't safe because an airplane is likely to hit them. Children may also worry about their family's financial situation if they hear parents voicing concerns. Teenagers may share some of these concerns, but with an added worry that they could be drafted into the military now that we are engaged in a war that may take years to win.

Fear, loss of control, instability and insecurity can cause a great deal of stress in children, especially when the adults around them are having trouble coming to terms with their own reactions.

Children who survived, witnessed, watched or found out about the World Trade Center disaster were probably as stressed out about it as you or I. They can show the effects of that stress in a variety of ways. Here's what you might expect.

Preschoolers	Clinginess, bedwetting, soiling of underwear, thumb sucking
Elementary school children	Clinginess, nightmares, behavior problems (aggressiveness, fighting), trouble with schoolwork, moodiness, headaches, stomach-aches, wheezing, rash
Adolescents	Headaches, stomach-aches, fatigue, social isolation, drug/alcohol use, rashes, diarrhea, sweating, insomnia, trouble concentrating, unexplained physical complaints or pains, aggressive behavior, eating disorders

Children suffering from post-traumatic stress disorder (PTSD) have similar symptoms, which should come as no surprise. According to the National Center for Post-Traumatic Stress Disorder, "The diagnosis of PTSD requires that an individual experience an event that involves a threat to one's own or another's life or physical integrity and that they respond with intense fear, helplessness or horror."[6] By that definition, we are all probably at risk for developing some PTSD symptoms. Although few studies of PTSD in children are available, existing research indicates that 77 percent of children and adolescents exposed to a school shooting and 35 percent of urban youth exposed to community violence develop PTSD.[7]

We don't want our children to become part of these statistics. We need to look out for the signs and symptoms of posttraumatic stress.

A 9-1-1 for 9/11

Knowing what to do or say to your children after a traumatic event is not always easy. Let's face it, this territory is new for most of us. Terrorism, threats and safety concerns used to be something that happened to "them" in some faraway country. We are entirely unprepared to deal with this new reality, but deal with it we must, or our children will suffer.

We can help our children through uncertain and chaotic times. As I learned with my young children, you almost certainly can't keep them from finding out about the World Trade Center attacks, anthrax scares, plane crashes or threats of more terrorism. Kids are way too smart for that. In fact, if you try to hide the truth you may do more harm than good. You can, however, shape the way they interpret the information they receive. Parents take on many roles in our child's life; in this case, we become spin doctors.

Kids need time to express their feelings, which is part of the cathartic process after a traumatic event. Younger children, especially those whose vocabulary is not sophisticated enough to deal with a trauma of this proportion (and whose really is?), may be clingy. Let them cling. Sometimes a hug is worth more than a thousand words.

Letting children draw—art therapy—is another

form of catharsis that may help children work through their fears. Although I was initially horrified when I saw Jacob's drawings of the disaster, I quickly realized that art was his way of expressing himself without letting down his six-year-old boy, macho, nothing-can-hurt-me, becoming-independent exterior.

Children old enough to speak will probably also need to talk about their feelings. Your response should be age-appropriate for the child. Grade-school children may have questions about the disaster. Use simple, clear language to answer their questions. Don't lie to them or tell them there's nothing to worry about, but don't tell them more than they want to hear. Trying to put your child's feelings into words may also help. Try something like, "It's so sad that all those people died when the buildings fell down," or "It's normal to be scared after seeing those planes crash." Don't make light of the situation because your children will see right through you. Also do not make promises you can't keep. If you tell a child, "Don't worry, that won't happen again," and another terrorist crashes a plane into a building, your child's trust may end up in ruins.

The situation may be reversed in adolescents and teenagers. They may play down their concerns. You should encourage them to talk about their feelings. Older children who repress fear often act out and misbehave. They may also be more susceptible to depression.

One sixteen-year-old girl I heard about was profoundly affected by the events of September 11, but she tried to ignore her fear and insecurity. When her parents tried to talk to her about the attacks, she told them, "I'm fine. I just want things to go back to normal." She tried to pretend they were. A couple of weeks later, she started complaining of vague aches and pains over her entire body. First her legs hurt, then her arms and back took turns hurting. She also became very tired. Her doctor examined her and took blood tests and X-rays. They were all normal. The doctor's diagnosis: posttraumatic stress disorder. The girl's parents agreed. She is now in counseling to deal with her anxiety.

When I tell parents this story, some of them flinch. As one father asked, "How am I supposed to help my child through this when I can barely comprehend it, much less deal with it myself?"

Avoiding tough issues is not part of the parental job description. If you are having trouble dealing with the traumatic events yourself, communicating that trouble to an older, mature child may be okay. He will instinctively know anyway. However, don't lay all of your psychological burdens on him. Instead, use your feelings to show him that what he is going through is normal, and that healing will be possible over time.[8]

Some psychologists also suggest you give your child a sense of control over the situation. For example, nightmares and insomnia are quite common during a national crisis. If your child suffers from these symptoms, ask her, "What will make you feel better?" If she asks to sleep with you for a while, let her. Something as simple as reading an extra bedtime story could help. When you involve your children in the healing process, you help them recover the sense that they have some control over their lives.[9]

As part of being a spin doctor, you should try to monitor the flow of information your child receives. You can't stop children from talking to their friends.

Indeed, such communication is often part of the healing process. However, limiting your child's exposure to the media can be a good idea. In the immediate aftermath of the World Trade Center attacks, the twenty-four-hour-a-day television coverage (to which, I must admit, I contributed), and the repeated airing of the gruesome attack footage, nearly sank the entire country into a mass depression. We should not let that happen to our children. Keep young children from watching news broadcasts. I was told about one set of parents who came up with a slick way to do this without calling attention to their concern: they scheduled an activity like story time, or arts and crafts during the news.

My family substitutes other activities instead of watching the news. I don't even want my children watching *me* on television because so many of my reports these days are about bioterrorism, PTSD, the war, etc. However, my children are young and their lives are still (relatively) controllable. Limiting media exposure for older children and teenagers is harder. The most important thing you can do is monitor the amount and type of their exposure, especially the Internet. If what they are watching, reading or surfing seems to make them more anxious, you may need to step in and impose some limits on their activities. As children grow older, they will like your intervention less. However, your involvement may prevent chronic anxiety and depression.

There are other steps you can take.

- Stick to a routine as much as possible. All humans, especially children, find comfort in routines. They add to a sense of security.
- Do activities that reinforce the idea that one

person can make a difference in providing hope and healing. These kinds of activities include raising money to help victims' families or writing letters of support to survivors.

- Make sure your child eats a well-balanced diet and has plenty of opportunity to rest. These factors help children ward off the physical effects of stress.
- Find ways to show your kids you love them.

This book does not pretend to provide all the answers. However, I hope that it can help you help your children cope with the daily stress they will face in the aftermath of the attacks on our country. Some of these stresses are obvious and dramatic—a product of the new world disorder; others are more subtle—a result of the pressures we knowingly or unknowingly place on our children. In either case, stress can build up and have a devastating impact on a child as he or she grows up.

Every generation hopes that their children will live better lives than they did. That's the American way, the dream that continues to beckon to people the world over. September 11 does not change that dream; the events of fall 2001 only make the dream more difficult to achieve. I hope this book will contribute in some small way to keeping that dream alive for all of us parents.

TWO

STRESS, AMERICAN-STYLE

Terrorism is not the only factor parents have to worry about. The world around us is full of destabilizing factors, and many stresses are homegrown.

Denise was thirteen years old when she and her parents went on a trip to Orlando, Florida, with another family that had a sixteen-year-old son. Denise and the boy spent a lot of time together during the vacation. They ate meals, swam and rode the roller coasters together. Toward the end of the trip, whenever they were alone, the boy began to pressure Denise for sex. At first she resisted, but eventually she gave in to the pressure and performed oral sex on the boy.

When Denise returned home from vacation, she began to complain of heart palpitations. Her parents took her to see a cardiologist, who put her through a battery of exams and tests; her heart was normal. Her psyche wasn't. Denise was racked with guilt and worry about her sexual encounter. She eventually confided in her pediatrician, telling him that she was worried about contracting AIDS or venereal disease.

After testing negative for HIV, Denise's heart palpitations disappeared. Her parents never found out why their daughter's symptoms appeared, and disappeared, so suddenly.

Two teenaged boys in Colorado spent many of their high school days being picked on, teased and physically assaulted by their classmates. The boys found comfort and refuge in a group of about a dozen students who were also social outcasts.[1] They all bought floor-length "duster" jackets at a Western store, played violent computer shoot-em-up games like "Doom" and toyed with Nazi signs and symbols.

On April 20, 1999, just weeks before their high school graduation, the two boys, Eric Harris and Dylan Klebold, walked into school and opened fire with automatic weapons, killing fifteen of their Columbine High School classmates before turning their guns on themselves.

According to some surveys, 15 percent of high school students have a drinking problem; one-third of schoolchildren under eighteen use illegal drugs; students carry nearly three hundred thousand guns to school each day; each year, more than 1 million teenaged girls become pregnant and almost two thousand teenagers kill themselves.[2]

Being a kid is not easy. There are raging hormones, sibling rivalries and family breakups. A lot of us faced these kinds of issues when we were growing up. Now we get to watch our children go through it. However, the burden of growing up today is greater than it was in our day. In addition to hormones and family problems, our children have to worry about societal pressures like sex, drugs, violence and the threat of AIDS.

The scariest part for many of us is that these societal pressures are out of our control. Our natural, parental instinct is to shield our children from the evils of the world, which is impossible, of course, but we don't stop trying. We are like Sisyphus, who was condemned by the gods to ceaselessly roll a rock to the top of a mountain, only to have the stone roll back down to the bottom. We can attempt to shelter our kids from the pressures of the world, but the pressure may eventually overwhelm our efforts.

Are you depressed yet? Don't be. Every generation has worried about the influence of culture on kids. Our parents worried about marijuana and rock and roll; their parents worried about jazz and J. D. Salinger. The "good old days" never really existed. The concept is just a fiction we've invented in a haze of hindsight.

And yet, and yet . . .

Our children certainly seem to be exposed earlier and more constantly to negative influences. Our society has become more violent; news reports of children gunning down other children have become so commonplace that they rarely even shock us anymore. Television shows, movies, and computer and video shoot-em-up games desensitize our children to violence with their graphic depictions of death and destruction. Music lyrics glorify violence and the exploitation of women. Indeed, we've come a long way from the pelvic gyrating of Elvis Presley to the misogynistic rap lyrics of Eminem.

Still Hurried

I was playing outside with my children not too long ago when we heard a song blaring from the radio next door. No sooner did the chorus start when I heard my then three-year-old daughter, Becca, start to sing, "Oops, I did it again. I played with your heart. . . ." She didn't know the rest of the lyrics to the song, but images of her wearing a belly shirt and dancing seductively, à la Britney Spears, immediately ran through my mind. I was horrified. Spears sings, "I'm not that innocent," but I'd like Becca (and my two sons) to be innocent for as long as possible.

A child's innocence is comforting, almost reassuring, reminding us that life is more than just the pursuit of money, fame, power or sexual conquest. When we peer into our child's innocent eyes, we catch a glimpse of our own innocence, or what's left of it. That insight gives us palpable hope for the future, enabling us to see the world anew, as if we were looking at it for the first time.

Society forcing children to shed their innocence before they are ready is a shame. Yet that's precisely what happens. Hurrying influences are all around us: music videos, alcohol and tobacco ads, sexy magazine covers, make-up sets for young girls, and revealing fashions. Hundreds of influences subtly and not so subtly push our children to grow up faster than they normally would.

This point was driven home when my son was five years old. He was watching a show on the Cartoon Network (we allow our children a maximum of one hour of television a day, if they watch it at all), when a commercial came on with an announcer saying, "Is your child embarrassed about not being able to read?" The ad was for some kind of phonics game that was "guaranteed" to teach children to read. Jacob had just started kindergarten and was beginning to show an interest in learning to read, a normal developmental level for a child his age. Yet when the ad was over, he turned to us and asked, "How come I can't read?" Isn't that just the kind of self-esteem-building a child watching the Cartoon Network needs?

That type of hurrying influence is present in our society almost everywhere we look, and that's only one small example. We're not just hurrying kids to read; we're hurrying them to play sports, to be fashionable, to be beautiful. Whether we realize it or not, our culture is turning our children into mini-adults.

Psychologist Margot Maine says, "Children grow up exposed to an incredible amount of sexuality, violence and sophistication that their little minds can't handle. . . . Wearing clothes in a certain fashion and being very sexual at young ages is something we're seeing more and more frequently."[3]

One mother named Digna sees firsthand the influence teen idols, like Britney Spears and Christina Aguilera, have over her twelve-year-old daughter, Amanda. The mother and daughter constantly bargain over how much lipstick and eye shadow Amanda can wear. "They don't want to be kids anymore," says Digna. "They want to be adults. They want to skip their teenage years and go right to adulthood."[4]

Parents constantly battle the media colossus. Everywhere children turn, they are exposed to idealized images of adult beauty, sexuality and "coolness." Just look at the cover of any teen magazine. You will almost certainly see a beautiful, impossibly thin female staring out at you. She represents American society's ideal of the perfect physical specimen, and many of our kids aspire to achieve that ideal. Author Naomi Wolf calls this concept "the beauty myth," the belief that one cannot be truly happy without being beautiful. Children are especially susceptible to this myth. Most of them don't realize that their favorite model or actress probably only looks "perfect" because of cosmetic surgery, airbrushing and a starvation diet.

Psychology Today has conducted surveys on how people feel about the appearance of their bodies. In 1972, 23 percent of American women were unhappy with their appearance; by 1997, that figure had risen to 56 percent.[5] If adults subscribe to the beauty myth, should we be surprised that our children do, too?

Dr. Paula Moynahan, a prominent New York City plastic surgeon, says, "The obsession by teens for physical perfection is motivated by peer pressure. However, it is influenced by the modern media's unceasing barrage of messages, whether in print, over the Internet or in various advertisements and movies. Consequently, the pressure to conform to a superimposed ideal is relentless and omnipresent."[6]

What these children aspire to is a mirage; still, they try. Children as young as thirteen years old are being nipped, tucked, sculpted and augmented at alarming rates. The American Society of Plastic Surgeons (ASPS) says surgeons performed 24,623 cosmetic procedures on teenagers in 1998, representing approximately 2 percent of all cosmetic operations performed in the United States. Nose jobs are the most common plastic surgery performed on teens, followed by otoplasty (corrective surgery for protruding ears), breast augmentation, breast reduction, chin implants and liposuction.

Surgery is not the only way children chase the beauty myth. About 1 percent of female adolescents have an eating disorder, and some children are starving themselves to death. One of these girls described her struggle poignantly.

Anorexia: the deadly result of a nation obsessed with impossible thinness.

I am anorexic.

Last year, I was in grade seven and fiddled with an eating disorder for a few months, but I'm not sure what happened. Somehow, I was eating, although surely not healthy. I was never a full-blown anorexic then.

I am anorexic.

In March '99, this year, I starved for a week and dropped a couple of pounds. The next week, I was up two pounds and then down and up and down.

I am anorexic.

In April, I starved for nearly the entire month, with the binges I couldn't resist and then the guilt. I started seeing a nutritionist—who's great.

I am anorexic.

Now it's the beginning of May and I spent the weekend on a total junk food binge. Today, I starved and had about 570 calories as of 7:10 P.M. This is dangerous and if I continue, I will start fainting, and if I really continue, I will die.

I am anorexic. . . .[7]

Children who pursue unrealistic goals are doomed to fail. Yet ubiquitous forces in our society continually push children to be thinner, "older," more beautiful, more popular and sexier. The prevailing culture entices children to try to attain the unattainable. Is it surprising that our children are physically and emotionally burned out? They are hurrying down a dead-end road.

Dr. David Elkind was one of the first people to detail this trend in his classic book *The Hurried Child:* "Psychologists and psychiatrists recognize that emotions and feelings are the most complex and intricate part of development. Feelings and emotions have their own timing and rhythm and cannot be hurried. Young teenagers may look and behave like adults, but they usually don't feel like adults. . . . Growing up emotionally is complicated and difficult under any circumstances but may be especially so when children's behavior and appearance speak 'adult' while their feelings cry 'child.'"[8]

We end up with psychologically conflicted children. Counselor Carleton Kendrick says, "Twenty years ago, I didn't see children in my therapy practice who resembled burned out, career-driven, Type A adults. I didn't see kids with chronic stress-related headaches, stomachaches and free-floating anxiety. I do now. Lots of 'em—little kids, big kids, kindergartners . . . I expect any day now to see a virtual reality childhood marketed."[9]

At least a virtual reality childhood would be better than no childhood at all. When our children are hurried into adulthood, they are also hurried into having adult problems.

Michael was a fourteen-year-old boy who loved heavy metal music. His room was covered with posters of tattoo-laden men sporting long hair and guitars, often accompanied by scantily clad women in provocative poses. Michael idolized and tried to emulate his favorite rockers. He started wearing tattered clothes and growing his hair long, all with the tacit approval of his parents. They saw a lot of the other boys in the neighborhood doing it and didn't want Michael to be ostracized. These baby-boomers also wanted their kids to think they were cool, so they indulged Michael's interests, as long as he kept his grades up.

One day, Michael and a friend were in his room listening to music and drawing fake tattoos on each other's arms to mimic their heroes. When they were done, they marveled at how much they looked like heavy metal icons. Only one thing was missing, they agreed: body piercing. Michael knew his parents would never allow him to get his ear pierced, so he decided to do it himself. His friend "sterilized" a sewing needle with a lighted match, then jabbed the needle through the skin of his left ear. Michael bent a piece of metal into a circle and inserted it into his newly pierced ear.

Ten hours later, Michael woke up in the middle of the night with fever and shaking chills. When his parents saw him, they noticed a large area of redness and swelling around the left ear, extending onto the left side of the face. As they called the doctor, Michael's condition worsened, almost by the minute. He complained of feeling weak and dizzy and was unable to stand. His parents called 911, and within minutes he was taken by ambulance to the local emergency room. In the ER, Michael's blood pressure dropped dangerously low, and he began to drift in and out of consciousness. The doctors diagnosed toxic shock syndrome, brought on by an infection at the site of the newly pierced ear, and instituted life-saving treatments that eventually brought Michael's infection under control.

Michael had almost lost his life because he was trying to hurry himself from a fourteen-year-old into an adult rocker, but such an incident is not news-worthy. Michael did what kids have been doing for decades, trying to make themselves into the next Elvis Presley, James Dean or Michael Jackson. However, the stakes are higher today than they were ten, twenty or more years ago. As images of sex and violence become more pervasive in our society, rock stars, movie idols and other media icons find shock-ing or rebelling more and more difficult. The further they go, the more they desensitize society to these destructive images, and the more dangerous their influence on our children. Consider: People freaked out when Elvis Presley shook his hips on stage. Now the married former president of the United States can receive oral sex in the Oval Office from an intern nearly his daughter's age, and half of the population barely raises an eyebrow.

Forbidden Fruit

Many parents have told me that they "don't let" their kids watch violent television shows or movies, play video games where the object is to kill someone (or something), or listen to violent music. We should applaud these parents for their efforts, but they are probably deluding themselves. We cannot watch our children twenty-four hours a day, seven days a week. They will watch television, go to the movies, listen to music, read magazines and play computer games whether we like it or not. In fact, the average

American child spends as much as twenty-eight hours a week watching television and typically at least an hour a day playing video games or surfing the Internet. Children spend several more hours each week watching movies and videos and listening to music.

After all, even Adam and Eve in paradise rebelled against authority, and they were kicked out for their actions.

The media can provide positive influences or relief valves that allow our children to blow off steam or just relax. The wide variety of media can teach, encourage and even inspire, but too often, they have the opposite effect. The American Academy of Pediatrics (AAP) notes that more than a thousand studies "point overwhelmingly to a causal connection between media violence and aggressive behavior in some children. . . . Its effects are measurable and long lasting. Moreover, prolonged viewing of media violence can lead to emotional desensitization toward violence in real life."[10]

One example of this desensitization comes from professional wrestling. Despite the fact that the violence and aggression of professional wrestling are obviously fake, a recent study says teenage boys who watch a lot of it on television are more likely to slap, hit or sexually assault a girl on a date.[11] Indeed, one thirteen-year-old boy was recently convicted in the murder of a six-year-old girl; he had been performing wrestling moves on her that he learned by watching pro wrestling on television. The boy now faces the possibility of spending the rest of his life behind bars.

This desensitization to violence spills over into our schools. Eric Harris and Dylan Klebold weren't alone in feeling like social outcasts at school. More than half of kids ages eight to eleven and two-thirds of children ages twelve to fifteen say teasing and bullying are big problems in school.[12] As kids grow older, the problem becomes worse. Yet many of us think school is a place for our children to feel safe and stable, even while the world around them rocks with instability.

And how about sex? It's everywhere in our society, from movies to magazine covers to music lyrics. Our children can barely turn on the television without being bombarded by some reference to sex. The Kaiser Family Foundation found sexual content (talk about sex, flirting, kissing, intimate touching and depictions of intercourse) in 68 percent of the shows studied during the 1999 to 2000 television season, compared with 56 percent only two years earlier.[13] The study found that the number of teenagers depicted engaging in intercourse tripled to 9 percent, while only one in ten programs were found to emphasize sexual risks and responsibilities.

Our cultural outlets are so filled with sexuality that one in four teens said they learn a lot about pregnancy and birth control from the media. To compound the problem, studies have shown that parents are often hesitant to bring up difficult topics like sex, drugs, AIDS and violence. "Yet while those topics aren't addressed at home, even the younger kids say they are feeling the pressure at school. One third of ten- to eleven-year-olds called the pressure to have sex a 'big problem.'"[14] Maybe that's why the teen pregnancy rate in the United States, while dropping, is still the highest of any Western nation.

We can't control the record industry. We can't choose which movies Hollywood makes. We can't cure AIDS. We can't prevent random acts of violence. Those societal pressures will always be beyond our control. However, we must fight hard to keep these destabilizing forces from affecting our own children. Raising stable kids in an unstable world is a little like turning your home into an eye in the middle of the hurricane. The job is not easy, but if we fail, our children often suffer the consequences.

THREE

THE
PHYSICS OF STRESS

Marks's First Theory of Psychodynamics

So what's the big deal about stress, anyway? Why should we worry about it? What effect does it have on our children? These important questions, I believe, can be answered by, of all things, a variation of one of the principal laws of physics that govern the universe.

The First Law of Thermodynamics states that you can't create or destroy energy; you can only change its form. This principle is also known as the principle of conservation of energy. For example, when you put a log of wood into your fireplace, the log may eventually disappear into the fire, but its energy is converted into light and heat. Energy is neither created nor destroyed; the wood merely turns into fire.

I believe the same principle applies to stress. After all, Einstein's equation, $e=mc^2$, tells us that all living creatures consist of varying degrees of energy. When we are consciously or subconsciously subjected to stress energy, we can't simply destroy it. If we vent it through conversation, art, exercise or writing, we convert stress into a productive form of energy. To some extent, this conversion process forms the basis of treatments such as psychotherapy and art therapy. Even a good screaming episode once in a while can help vent negative stress energy that has built up over time.

However, because it cannot be destroyed, chronic stress energy that is not vented can be converted into harmful forms of energy that affect our bodily functions, causing chronic pain, asthma, rashes, an ineffective immune system and other physical symptoms. Suppressed stress energy may also be converted, through chemical changes in the brain, into psychological problems such as depression, anxiety and eating disorders.

I call this concept the First Law of Psychodynamics: The Conservation of Stress Energy. While no experimental proof exists (I don't even know how one could design an experiment or measure a precise amount of stress energy), ample practical experience is available to support this theory.

Take Eddie as an example. When he was seven years old, he began to complain of a gnawing, cramping pain in his stomach. His symptoms did not seem to fit the pattern of any specific disease, leaving both his parents and his pediatrician stumped as to the cause. A number of medical specialists saw him and offered various diagnoses, including acid reflux, stomach ulcers, irritable bowel syndrome, milk allergy, abdominal migraine and finally spastic colon.

After multiple tests and treatments failed to help, Eddie's parents felt desperate. As a last resort, they took him to a child psychologist, who quickly uncovered the source of Eddie's stomach pain. Eddie was feeling stressed by the pressure his parents put on him to perform at the top of his class in school. He was only entering third grade!

Eddie suffered unnecessarily because none of his medical doctors had ever thought to explore the possibility that psychological, not physical, factors were at the root of his symptoms. But shortly after Eddie and his parents started family counseling, Eddie's stomachaches disappeared—and he still did well in school. Once he began to talk about his feelings, the stress energy changed from a destructive to a constructive force in his life.

The connection between the mind and body is a mysterious one, but it exists, without a doubt. If you don't believe in this connection, just consider the last time you felt embarrassed. Chances are your faced flushed, you felt warm, and perhaps you even started sweating and your heart began to beat faster, all because of a single embarrassing thought. That thought caused a cascade of stress-related hormones and chemicals to rush into your bloodstream. As these substances spread throughout your body, they affected virtually every organ and cell they encountered: heart, kidneys, brain, blood vessels, lungs, eyes, intestines, immune system and sweat glands. The result was a chemical and hormonal hurricane that eventually engulfed a significant portion of your body.

How about this? We've all had nightmares. Sometimes a bad dream seems so real you would swear it was actually happening. You know what I mean: your heart races, you sweat, and when you awaken, you're temporarily disoriented before you realize you were just dreaming. However, while you were asleep, your mind felt the dream was reality and your body responded appropriately. Your thoughts led to physical reactions typical of stress.

Of course, a nightmare or an embarrassing situation is usually mild and short-lived. The storm passes quickly; your body rapidly regains its normal internal balance. However, repeated exposure to stress can be more dangerous. Research shows that our body responds to stress in the same manner as an allergy. The more we're exposed to stress, the more sensitized, or sensitive, to stress we become. After a while, even small amounts of stress can result in large physical changes.

One writer has observed that "by responding to the stress of everyday life with the same surge of biochemicals released during major threats, the body is slowly killing itself. The biochemical onslaught chips away at the immune system, opening the way to cancer, infection and disease. Hormones unleashed by stress eat at the digestive tract and lungs, promoting ulcers and asthma. Or they may weaken the heart, leading to strokes and heart disease."[1]

Evidence has been building for many years that stress can have a profound effect on adult health and the development of disease. For example, one study found that if you experience stress for more than a month, your risk of developing a cold more than doubles. Many of you experience this effect in your own lives. How often have you become sick when you felt like you were "burning the candle at both ends"? Even an imposing historical figure such as the late President Lyndon B. Johnson could fall prey to the effects of stress. Despite his stolid physical appearance and tough manner, President Johnson's bodily defenses gave out almost every time he found himself in a professional crisis. During his first congressional campaign, he suffered exhaustion followed by appendicitis. When he began serving in the U.S. House of Representatives he developed a "nervous rash" on his hands. During his first campaign for the U.S. Senate, he came down with pneumonia.

Some people call this "the stress syndrome" to denote the way that stress can affect the way our bodies function. A number of recent studies have demonstrated just how much of an impact stress has on our health.

- People in Amsterdam who experienced at least three "life-changing" events were more likely to develop diabetes than their less-stressed counterparts.
- When researchers gave people pills to raise their blood levels of the stress hormone cortisol, they did worse on memory tests than people who were given a placebo.
- One study showed that the stress of caring for a loved one with dementia can make you resistant to the protective effects of the flu vaccine.
- In another study, researchers deliberately made blisters on the arms of thirty-six women. Women who were under stress had lower concentrations of immune system chemicals in their wounds than women who were not under stress—and their wounds took 24 percent longer to heal.[2]

The list doesn't end there. Indeed, stress is believed to contribute to some of the leading causes of death in the U.S., including cancer, heart disease, accidental injuries, high blood pressure and substance abuse.

Stress also is linked to conditions as varied as asthma, multiple sclerosis, diabetes and stomach ulcers. One report even says that stress can lead to anatomical changes in the brain that may affect a person's mental health.[3]

Stress Is a Saber-Toothed Tiger

Picture a baseball player swinging at a pitch. If the ball strikes the top part of his bat, he will pop it up into the air for an easy out. If the ball strikes the bottom part of the bat, he will hit a ground ball and will likely be thrown out at first base. If, however, he hits the ball on the sweet spot of the bat, right in the middle, the ball will fly out into the outfield and possibly over the fence. A fraction of an inch can make the difference between a home run and an easy out.

Life, like hitting a baseball, is all about balance. When our body or mind loses its internal balance, we can feel stress. The medical term for this struggle to maintain harmony is *homeostasis* and is defined as "the maintenance of relatively stable internal physiological conditions . . . under fluctuating environmental conditions."[4]

Homeostasis is such a strong, driving force that the body is programmed to try to achieve it under all circumstances. For example, if you step on a nail, nerves on the bottom of your foot send electrical signals to your spinal cord. From there, the signals race up to your brain, where the flurry of electrical activity causes a release of chemicals that tell your body something is wrong; we experience it as pain. The whole process happens in a flash, but the end result of the change in your homeostasis is that you

immediately lift your foot off of the nail (and probably vent a little by using some choice language!)
before it causes real damage.

Stress is also the basis of the fight-or-flight
response. When you are threatened or in a sudden
crisis, your body immediately mobilizes all of its
energy, hormones and blood flow in the cause of sur-
vival. That overwhelming physiological response
allows you to run fast to escape the threat, or to
stand and fight like the dickens.

The fight-or-flight response, which is a remnant of
our days in the caves, allowed prehistoric men and
women to succeed as hunters and warriors in a hos-
tile and dangerous world. We may have evolved, but
the primitive fight-or-flight response is still with us.
Unfortunately, this physiological response that
evolved to protect us from saber-toothed tigers kicks
in to combat many of today's stresses, as if they were
life-threatening.

Here's the problem: when the fight-or-flight
response occurs periodically, the body has an opportunity to recover. When the danger is gone, the body
returns to homeostasis. Under chronic stress, the
constant release of hormones and neurochemicals
and the ongoing expenditure of energy wreak havoc
on the body, wearing down the body's defense mechanisms until they become exhausted and are unable
to maintain a state of internal harmony. A body that
can no longer resist stress begins to break down both
physically and psychologically. As one scientist says,
stress can drain energy from the functions of your
body that are essential to good health, such as fixing
damaged cells, fighting bacteria and viruses, and
replacing used-up brain chemicals. He says, "You
will 'hit the wall,' 'run out of gas.' If you continue,

permanent damage may be done. The body's fight to stay healthy in the face of the increased energy that you are expending is a major stress."[5]

One Washington, D.C., psychologist aptly described this chronic assault on the body: "Burnout is like trying to race a marathon, full speed, nonstop. Can anyone race twenty-six miles full speed, nonstop? Of course not. Even Olympic marathon runners must pace themselves. If not, the body parts will break down. And with burnout, over time, the mental apparatus also wears out."[6]

Thus, our need for homeostatic balance is as basic as our need for food, water, shelter and clothing. When we have balance in our lives, our bodies and minds function harmoniously. When our lives drift out of balance, we feel stress, and disease, depression or dysfunction often follow.

Children also need balance. Too often, though, their lives resemble ours: stress-filled, hectic, pressured, dangerous and unbalanced. They are subjected to many forces that tend to push them away from homeostasis. When those forces are unopposed, children can end up being pushed to physical or mental extremes, resulting in physical and psychological illness. One job of parents and adults in society is to help children maintain homeostasis in their lives. They need our help to achieve balance in the midst of the chaotic, pressure-filled society swirling around them.

Most adults were not born to be marathon runners. Neither were our children. But too often our children are forced into the race before they're ready. Is it any wonder that so many of our children are unable to complete life's marathon without suffering some sort of physical or psychological injury?

Stress and Kids

Most of the studies on stress and health have focused on adults. Those studies have demonstrated that burnout is an equal opportunity problem. Stress can affect the powerful and the disenfranchised, the bodybuilder and the ninety-eight-pound weakling.

Chronic stress, it turns out, can cause the same, if not more, damage in children as it does in adults. Some studies suggest that children may go through developmental periods during which exposure to stress is more damaging than in later years.[7] The earlier children are sensitized to stress, the more susceptible they may be to the effects of stress down the road. Some experts even believe that early life stress can cause permanent changes in the brain that may help create mental disorders later in life.[8]

Of course, totally protecting your child from stress is impossible. Even if you could, doing so wouldn't be a great idea. Children are going to face plenty of stress when they become adults; learning to deal with stress helps children grow up and mature. Stress can also motivate them to perform their best and accept new challenges. When I was playing on my high school basketball team, I felt butterflies before every game. The surge of adrenaline coursing through my bloodstream helped me prepare for the contest. That nervous feeling may help for a few minutes before a game.

No one wants to feel butterflies in their stomach or performance anxiety forever, but that's what chronic stress is like. The effects of chronic stress on children can be seen in either the physical, emotional or psychological dimensions. Research is now demonstrating that stress affects the health of our children more than we ever thought possible.

- One out of three American children suffers from stress-related illnesses such as headaches, stomachaches, chest pain, dizziness and wheezing.
- "Type A" children have higher blood cholesterol levels than other children, putting them at higher risk for heart disease.
- Stressed-out children have been shown to get more colds and flus than "non-stressed" children. Research has found that these stressed children have lower levels of virus-fighting antibodies in their upper respiratory tracts.[9]
- Recurrent abdominal pain due to stress is a common complaint in general pediatric and gastroenterology clinics.[10, 11]
- Stress may be responsible for chronic muscle or joint pain in many preadolescents.[12]
- Children who are more biologically sensitive to stress are ill more often than their peers. However, when their lives are relatively stress free, they are sick much less frequently.[13]
- Some children in stressful environments may actually suffer growth failure, sometimes called "psychosocial dwarfism." When the child with stress-related growth failure is removed from the stressful environment, he begins to grow normally again.[14]
- Students given the hepatitis-B vaccine during stressful periods of time, such as studying for exams, make fewer antibodies against hepatitis-B than those vaccinated when they aren't under stress.[15]

- "By four or five years old, the brains of stressed kids can start to look an awful lot like the brains of stressed adults, with increased levels of adrenaline and cortisol, the twitchy chemicals that fuel the body's fight-or-flight response. Keep the brain on edge long enough, and the changes become long-lasting, making learning harder as kids get older."[16]

Parents should be aware, however, that even if their child doesn't show any signs or symptoms of stress, she's not out of the woods. Some research shows that early stress may only catch up with a child when she reaches adulthood. Dr. David Elkind says, "Excessive stress in childhood can have life-long effects by producing patterns of stress reaction that stay with the young person throughout life."[17]

A Tale of Two Kiddies

"We hold these truths to be self-evident, that all men are created equal. . . ." Thomas Jefferson's poetic and inspiring words embodied the force behind the American Revolutionary War. The only problem is, they are not true. Contrary to popular belief and political correctness, we are not all created equal. Each of us, including our children, is unique. People differ in height, hair color, temperament and so many other characteristics. Like adults, children differ in the way they respond to stress. Some kids can go to school all day, compete in two sports, take piano lessons, maintain good grades and be none the worse for wear. Other children, who develop physical, psychological or behavioral problems under much less stressful conditions, are simply more vulnerable to stress.

Joshua Rosenfeld was twelve years old when his concerned parents first brought him to my office at the New England Center for Headache. After we introduced ourselves, I began to ask Joshua about his headaches. As he was formulating an answer to my first question, though, his mother cut him off.

"Dr. Marks," she said, "Josh is a very bright child, a straight-A student, but we're worried that these headaches are going to interfere with his school-work. He's going to take AP [advanced placement] courses in a few years, and we don't want his headaches to keep him from doing well."

Advanced placement courses at twelve years of age? By my calculations, Joshua had about four years before walking into his first AP classroom. The fact that his parents were already worried was a red flag.

I waited for Mrs. Rosenfeld to finish, then turned my attention back to Joshua and repeated the question.

"What do your headaches feel like?"

"They're all around his head and in his temples," his mom blurted, again before he had the chance to describe his own symptoms.

When I was alone with Joshua in the exam room I learned the true reason for his headaches. Once he began to speak, the words and tears poured out of him.

His parents were highly educated people who held prestigious jobs in their native country. When they were forced to move to the United States for political reasons, they also left their professional lives behind. Mr. Rosenfeld was now a maintenance worker; his wife worked as an assistant at a preschool. Neither of them was happy with the status quo, and like so many immigrants over the years, their hopes for success in America devolved onto their children.

As the eldest son, Joshua carried the heavier burden. He was, indeed, a very bright child, but his parents did not want to leave anything to chance. They enrolled him in a variety of activities designed to make him an academic star: Chinese language courses, classical piano lessons, science classes at the local museum, and a private math tutor to help him "get a jump on algebra."

"I wouldn't mind taking any of the classes alone," he explained as I tapped on his knee with my reflex hammer, "but I just can't handle them all and do my schoolwork at the same time."

"Have you discussed this with your parents?" I asked.

"Yes, but they won't listen. They say I need to do these things if I'm going to be something one day. My dad always says to me, 'Do you want to be a maintenance worker like me when you grow up?' When I say, 'No,' he says, 'Well, that's why your mother and I want you to continue your classes. We know it's hard, but you'll thank us one day.'"

I finished the neurological exam and stood in front of Joshua. He was upset from the conversation, yet he also looked relieved to have unburdened himself.

"Have you ever just told them 'no'? Or that you wanted a day off to play baseball or hang out and do nothing?" I asked.

"I've tried. It's no use. They won't even let me play baseball. They think it's a stupid game that takes away from my studies. And God forbid I should bring home a report card with anything but As. I probably wouldn't be allowed to have any fun at all."

When Joshua and I returned to my office and rejoined his family, I continued taking his medical history. I routinely asked about foods, weather changes and other environmental factors that can affect headaches, but I had already made a diagnosis. His headaches clearly resulted from stress. Joshua was simply wilting under the pressure of trying to live up to his parents' unrealistic expectations.

He also had a ten-year-old brother who was subjected to parental pressure to "succeed." However, Joshua's brother did not suffer from headaches or any other chronic physical or psychological ailment. The two lived in the same house with the same parents, yet the effects of stress on each couldn't have been more different. Of course, it's possible that in the next few years his brother will also develop symptoms of burnout. Still, the fact that he has remained symptom-free until now is a testament to how children respond to stress differently.

The difference between Joshua and his brother may lie in their genes. Researchers have been able to breed strains of rats that respond very differently to stress. One strain, called Fischer rats, pours out stress hormones when they're exposed to even small amounts of stress. Another strain, called Lewis rats, produces very little stress hormone no matter what happens to them.[18]

Humans aren't rats (most aren't, anyway), but genetics undoubtedly plays a role in our sensitivity to stress. We all share the same biological mechanism for responding to stress, but our genes may determine, at least in part, how and when that mechanism is activated.

Some research found that between 15 and 20 percent of children three to eight years old had exaggerated biological responses to stressful events. When these children were stressed, they had higher-than-normal changes in blood pressure and heart rates and higher levels of stress hormones released into their bloodstream. Interestingly, these children were also more likely to develop respiratory infections and behavioral problems.[19,20] However, research also indicates that the number of infections and behavioral problems decreased when the children were exposed to less stress. The more stable their world, the less likely they were to become ill!

The different ways that people respond to stress may even be preprogrammed into their cells. One study has demonstrated that people can be separated into "high reactors" and "low reactors," based on the way their immune cells react to stress; the number of "killer" lymphocytes in the blood increased when high reactors were stressed, but stayed the same in low reactors.[21]

Parents and researchers have debated the relative importance of nature and nurture for decades. Some say genetics is destiny; others say that development is all about upbringing. The truth probably lies somewhere in between. Studies like those cited above show how important heredity is. So does the Human Genome Project, the results of which we are just beginning to see. Scientists have identified thirty-five thousand or so genes in the human genome and have no idea what the majority of those genes do. Yet, researchers have already found genes that can make a person more susceptible to developing Alzheimer's disease,[22] and post-traumatic stress disorder,[23] as well as a host of other medical conditions.

We've all seen the power of genetics. Many of us remember the runner Jim Fixx, whose 1977 best-selling book, *The Complete Book of Running,* is credited with launching America's fitness revolution. Unfortunately, Mr. Fitness died of a heart attack at age fifty-two while running. On the other hand, most of us know at least one chain-smoker or heavy drinker who has lived to be eighty or ninety years old. Some people are partially doomed by genetics, and others are blessed.

I have a theory that I call the 80/20 Principle. I believe that 80 percent of who we are is genetically programmed meaning that some people are *more likely* to be sensitive to stress; some are *more likely* to be good in mathematics; some are *more likely* to develop heart disease when they are young; and some are *more likely* to weather the effect of nicotine or alcohol.

No scientific proof exists for my 80/20 Principle. Yet, in my experience as a clinician and a parent, the Principle holds true. And as scientists continue to unlock the human genome, each time they discover a gene for this or a gene for that, I grow more confident that the 80/20 Principle is legitimate. (The 80/20 split is just my best estimate based on clinical and practical observations. Perhaps the split is 70/30, 90/10, or some other fraction in between.)

Genetics is not necessarily destiny, however. Notice that I said some people are *more likely* to react a certain way than others. The 80/20 Principle means that we can affect the 20 percent of a person that is not "hard wired." In many cases, that 20 percent may make a crucial difference, perhaps a Type A kid could become more relaxed; maybe a nonanalytical child can improve his scores in math and science; a runner might live to sixty-two instead of fifty-two. The point is that parenting is still important, despite our children's genetic programming.

You can see the interplay between genetics and environment in the way children respond to stress. Their responses often depend on the importance they give to the "stressor." For example, someone told me the story of eight-year-old identical twin sisters, Julie and Chris. Their parents packed their schedules with a lot of after-school activities, including piano lessons, ballet and soccer. Julie loved running back and forth between school, home and her daily activities. Sometimes she would even complain to her parents about being bored during the few occasions when she had an hour or two of free time. She thrived on the frenetic pace of her young life.

Chris, on the other hand, reacted very differently. She tried to keep up with her twin sister, but eventually developed chronic headaches that kept her home on many days. After months of being sick, Chris's parents cut back on her extracurricular activities since, as they told her, she "wasn't going anyway." Without knowing it, Chris's parents had stumbled onto the cure for her headaches. As the demands on her time decreased, so did her head pain.

Chris and Julie shared the same set of genes (they are identical twins) and the same hectic schedule. Despite that, they responded to stress very differently. One probable explanation is that each had a different perception of how stressful their hectic schedules were.

Determining how our children gauge stress is very difficult. Talking to them is the best approach, but many children won't, or can't, express their inner feelings. Therefore, we are often left to simply observe the way our children react to stressful situations. If they become emotional, withdrawn or sick, or their behavior changes in any way, we can probably assume that they perceive an event or circumstance as stressful. If they don't demonstrate any of those behavioral or physical changes, then that which we perceive as being stressful may not have much of an impact on their psyche.

A child's perception of stress, combined with his genetically determined responsiveness to stress, helps to determine how susceptible he is to it. But Dr. Esther Sternberg, author of *The Balance Within: The Science Connecting Health and Emotions,* points out that interpersonal relationships are also important in a person's susceptibility to stress. She writes, "[interpersonal relationships can] in some cases contribute to, and in other cases . . . buffer us from stress. In many ways, relationships can be the most powerful stressors that most people will encounter in their waking, working lives. And they can be the greatest soothers, too."[24]

In a sense, parents need to become psychophysicists.[25] If we understand the First Law of Psychodynamics, we can begin to help our children convert negative energy into a different, more positive and healthier form.

PART II

The World
Within

Four

Home Is Where the Stress Is

Children like stability. In fact, they thrive on it, which makes sense. When the world approaches homeostasis, a child finds it easier to achieve internal homeostasis. In reality, though, the world usually comes closer to chaos than homeostasis, which is why parents must do their best to create a stable, low-stress environment within their households. The problem is that many of us unwittingly add to our children's stress by the choices we make and the lives we lead.

Choices

Let's face it. Most people are caught up—stressed out and overworked—in life's rat race, and our psychological and physical health suffer. Drs. Meyer Friedman and Ray Rosenman recognized this fact more than twenty years ago when they defined the Type A personality. They wrote, "The Type A man incessantly strives to accomplish too much or to participate in too many events in the amount of time he allots for these purposes. . . . [He has] a failure to perceive, or perhaps worse, to accept the simple fact that a man's time can be exhausted by his activities.

As a consequence, he never ceases trying to 'stuff' more and more events in his constantly shrinking reserves of time."[1]

Ironically, one of the bestselling books over the last few years deals with life's rat race. The phenomenal success of *Tuesdays with Morrie* by Mitch Albom (Doubleday, 1997) shows that millions of adults recognize the destructive effects of today's fast-paced, high-pressure lifestyle. People thirst for ways to regain a more balanced perspective.

Many of the same adults may not understand that the rat race they seek to avoid also has a negative impact on their children. Indeed, they ignore one of the most important lessons of the book. As Morrie Schwartz, the main character in *Tuesdays with Morrie,* said while he was slowly dying from Lou Gehrig's disease, "We've got a form of brainwashing going on in our country. . . . *More is good. More is good.* We repeat it—and have it repeated to us—over and over until nobody bothers to even think otherwise. The average person is so fogged up by all this, he has no perspective [of] what's really important anymore." (italics in original).

What's happened is that we've become caught up in a narrow definition of success: wealth, productivity, prestige and celebrity. Worse than that, we've projected these warped and artificial notions of success onto our children. In the process, we've blurred the line between childhood and adulthood; with that situation comes adult-sized problems for our children.

The pursuit of "more" is the most common reason for burnout. We want more money, more power and more recognition, and in the process of that pursuit we often become overscheduled and sleep deprived. We have come to accept that this state of functioning is normal. Thus, we think nothing of subjecting our children to the same lifestyle. We fail to recognize that our own lives are often dysfunctional or unhealthy, so seeing that condition in our children is difficult.

Not only do we want more for ourselves, we want more for our children: more education, more stimulation, more toys and more opportunities. These desires are natural. Every generation wants to make their children's lives better than their own. Parents in prior generations worked hard to save enough money to send their children to college so that they, in turn, wouldn't have to struggle in the same way they did.

I remember how proud my parents were on the day I graduated from medical school. These two people, each of whom only had a high school education, sat in the audience beaming as their eldest son walked onto the stage to accept his diploma. They had worked their whole lives so that I would have opportunities that were unimaginable for them. Forget about the fact that I had to have massive amounts of financial aid to arrive at the point of graduation; I could never have done it without their support and encouragement.

My parents never pushed me to go to medical school. They didn't enroll me in after-school enrichment courses or set me up with a science tutor. My free time was just that, free. There were no play dates when I was young. We had never heard of them. When I was older, my chief after-school activity was playing catch or shooting baskets with my friends in the neighborhood. In the summer, when I wasn't working at McDonald's, I could usually be found on the beaches of Southern California.

My free time, and that of my friends, was actually free, not a designed or scheduled time. However, my parents and many others in their generation knew that kids need time to be kids. Parents didn't need advice books to teach them this lesson. Nor could many of the families have afforded tutors and multiple extracurricular activities even if they had desired them.

How times have changed. More of us middle- and upper-middle-class parents have enough money to educate our children and provide them with material comforts than might have been conceivable a generation earlier. We have pop psychologists instructing us on how to raise "high-achieving" kids. We're surrounded by books like *Magic Trees of the Mind: How to Nurture Your Child's Intelligence, Creativity, and Healthy Emotions from Birth Through Adolescence; 125 Brain Games for Babies;* and *How to Increase Your Child's Verbal Intelligence: The Groundbreaking Language Wise Method.* We read magazines like *Parenting, Child* and *Scholastic Parent and Child.* No wonder many parents feel concerned about their child's future chances of success.

To overcome our own fears, we engage in what Dr. Alvin Rosenfeld and Nicole Wise call "hyper-parenting": Many of us just don't know when to say "enough is enough." "We know we are doing too much for our kids, but don't know where it might be okay to cut back, especially since every time we pick up the paper, turn on the news, or try to lose ourselves in the pages of a magazine, someone else is adding something new to the list of things we are supposed to be doing for our children to make sure they turn out right."[2]

Despite this, our parents' instincts are proving to

be better than our penchant for programmed parenting. By letting us have free time, many of our parents gave us the opportunity to learn how to blow off steam. By letting us play on neighborhood ball fields, they helped us to enjoy our games. By nurturing our curiosity and letting us explore the world, they prepared us for lifelong learning. Unfortunately, many parents today have forgotten the lessons of our own childhoods.

Good Intentions, Bad Results

The community I live in is filled with parents who push their kids beyond all reasonable expectations. I know many of these parents personally. They are not bad people or unfit parents. Most of them do it because they want the best for their children, but the road to burnout is paved with good intentions.

Many of today's parents started down this ill-fated road in the late 1980s and early 1990s, when economic uncertainty fueled competition to have their children admitted to the top colleges so they could eventually land high-paying jobs. Psychologist John Friel, coauthor of *The 7 Worst Things Good Parents Do* (Health Communications, Inc., 1999), says, "Parents and school counselors and teachers got really panicky about their kids getting into good colleges and then getting good jobs. When the job market was bad, that was a very important thing to worry about.

"One of the things people started pushing on their kids was extracurricular activities, building up their resumes so they could get into a school. I think it was a worthwhile solution to an immediate problem, but it then took on a life of its own."[3]

Landing a good job, making money and being the best are important goals in an economically competitive world, but they are not the only ends worth pursuing. They may not even be the most important. Yet many people have buried any other goals for our children—like happiness, self-confidence and emotional health—under an avalanche of activities designed to produce superchildren. As one researcher at the University of Medicine and Dentistry in New Jersey has said, "Many parents' expectations of their children are very high because they are afraid of how competitive the world is right now and they're concerned for their kids' future."[4]

Children today also have more opportunities. Computers, "power learning courses," parenting consultants, a myriad of lessons and organized after-school activities now take up a lot of what used to be free time. Not wanting to take advantage of all these opportunities is hard. After all, every parent wants to feel that they're doing everything they can for their child. Many families have more money now that enables them to do it.

In one recent survey, 91 percent of children from wealthy families received music, art or dance lessons, 87 percent attended summer camp, and 86 percent had sports lessons.[5] We often hear that money affords a person more leisure time, but for many children, their parents' affluence is running them ragged.

The wealthy are by no means the only ones whose good intentions lead them to push their kids too hard. All of us are susceptible to the seduction of success. "Affluenza" is not just an affliction of the affluent. The truth is that all the activities, lessons and instruction may make us parents feel better, but they're not going to make our children super-children. More likely, this scheduled hyperactivity will make them grow them up to be like us: over-stressed, overworked, sleep deprived, mentally and physically unhealthy, and often unhappy.

John P. was one such child. When I first saw him, he was seven years old, with curly blond hair and pale blue eyes. John's parents had dragged him from doctor to doctor in an attempt to get rid of his chronic headaches. He had been on medicines, special diets and herbs. He had even seen a psychologist. Nothing worked because no one had identified the underlying cause of his pain.

John's problem quickly became obvious to me. His lifestyle was more hectic than most of the adults I know: soccer practice twice a week, soccer games once a week, weekly guitar lessons and karate classes, and very often, two play dates each week. John said he loved each of these activities, but he seemed to lack enthusiasm and energy. In short, he was burning out.

Many adult patients respond the same way. When they are stressed, their headaches get worse. They get stomachaches, feel depressed, lose their tempers or complain of chronic fatigue. Many doctors recognize this syndrome in adults. Advice like "take it easy," "cut back on your work load," "take some time off" and "slow down" is commonly given to adult burnouts. In children, however, doctors and psychologists sometimes miss the diagnosis because they don't ask about the child's lifestyle or schedule. Asking the right questions is crucial.

John's parents had no idea that his schedule could be harmful. They thought they were doing the right thing for him. Eventually, however, they agreed to limit their son to no more than two activities a week. A month after implementing this policy, they called to tell me that John's headaches had virtually disappeared.

John's parents hadn't overscheduled their son on purpose. John had told them repeatedly that he liked soccer. He was also good at it, so they encouraged him. How many of us would have done differently? When your child displays a particular talent, wanting to nurture it is only natural.

On the contrary, if you feel that your child lags "behind" his friends in a certain skill, your first instinct is usually to do whatever it takes to "bring him up to speed": flashcards, the Phonics Game, math tutors or private skating lessons might be sought.

So, whether a child is behind or ahead, enthusiastic or inexperienced, our natural inclination is to have her do more, more, more. Unfortunately, like most things in life, too much of a good thing can be bad for you.

Keeping Up with the Joneses

Of course, telling a parent to give their child time to relax and do nothing is not easy, especially when every other child is running from activity to activity. No one wants his or her child left behind.

Peer pressure is one of the most powerful forces responsible for making our children sick. "If little Johnny next door is doing it, my child must do it, too, or he'll fall behind." Child rearing can resemble an arms race. But instead of building nuclear weapons, this race is about whose child is smarter or stronger or faster or better prepared to compete in a cutthroat world.

I have felt this peer pressure myself. When I hear that one of my five-year-old son's friends takes piano lessons, has a private reading coach, is enrolled in a foreign language and is learning how to ski, I react like many other parents in the same situation. I ask myself if I'm putting my son at a disadvantage that'll catch up with him further on down the road. I forget the fact that he's a bright, happy kid who does well in school and makes friends easily. Instead, I become blinded by my own ambitions, insecurities and neuroses, and (temporarily, at least) insinuate them into my son's life.

Dr. Randy Weeks, a psychologist and director of the New England Institute for Behavioral Medicine, has counseled many overscheduled, stressed-out children. He says, "A piece of it is the insecurity of parents that if they're not keeping up with the Joneses, then they're not really fulfilling their role as parents. They're more interested in how many things they can give them than in how much time they can spend with them. Some of it is perhaps compensation. Mom and Dad may not be around, so they get their kid involved in five different things, but a lot of it is just so they can point and say, 'Look what a good parent I am.'"[6]

Dr. Marilyn Sorenson, a clinical psychologist in Portland, Oregon, and author of the book, *Breaking the Chain of Low Self-Esteem,* agrees that insecurity is a big part of what drives parents to try to keep up with the Joneses: "Comparison is really a big issue for people with low self-esteem. It's because they feel inadequate themselves. So they compare themselves with other people, with other parents, and they tend to look at the achievements, or lack of achievements, of their children as a reflection on them as a parent."[7]

When parenting becomes a competitive sport, children sometimes become little more than trophies, and parents will do almost anything to make sure that their trophy is the biggest and shiniest.

Trophy Kids

Melanie and Joseph Platt offer an example of insecure parents who see their kids as trophies. The Platts are a well-to-do couple living in the suburbs around a major city who inherited a successful business and a large sum of money. They lived the high life and never failed to let their friends know how much everything cost them and how many "important" friends they had. But according to one of their friends, through all the bravado seeped a sense of insecurity, as if the Platts never really felt they were as good as their peers.

They lived in a nice house with a tennis court on which their sons had been taking private tennis lessons since they were old enough to hold a racket. Despite this, the Platts decided to sign up their five-year-old son, Peter, for extra lessons at a local tennis club. These lessons consisted of a group of four five-year-olds taking turns trying to hit the ball back to an instructor. Since Peter was the only boy who had ever held a tennis racket before, he was the only one who could even make contact with the ball during the first couple of lessons.

Melanie made a point to phone the other mothers after lessons to apologize. She told one mother, "I hope Michael didn't feel too bad out there watching Peter hit all those balls." Needless to say, that mother was incredulous.

During one lesson, Melanie flew into a rage because the instructor made the boys do jumping jacks instead of hitting balls. She stormed up to the instructor and asked what was happening.

"How could you do that? I paid for Peter to be in a group where he could practice his hitting."

"I don't see a problem, Ma'am. So your son will hit a few less balls this week. Who cares? The kids are getting exercise and they're having fun," the instructor explained.

"Well, having fun may be good enough for some children," Melanie fumed, "but it's not for mine. Peter is a very good tennis player. He can beat seven- and eight-year-olds. I don't want his lessons to be watered down."

The mother who told me this story said that she and the rest of the moms in the group sat there, stunned, as Melanie took Peter's hand and led him to the club office to complain. But the next week, this same mother had the opportunity to ask Peter if he enjoyed playing tennis.

His response was not a simple "yes," or "it's fun," or anything you would expect from a child. Instead, Peter answered in words eerily similar to his mother's: "Well, I'm very good at it. I can beat seven- and eight-year-olds."

"But did you ask your mother if you could take lessons twice a week?" the woman asked.

"No. My mom makes me because I'm so good at it."

Forcing your child to play a sport because *you* like it (both Melanie and Joseph play tennis) and not because *he* likes it is the epitome of living vicariously through your child.

Dr. Sal Severe says that when we push our children too hard, we often have "leftover wishes from our own childhood, expectations our parents put on us, that we think we must put on kids, our own peer groups, our neighborhood.

"We live through our children. We measure ourselves based upon what they are doing."[8]

We may do this, in part, because in other ways that we measure ourselves, we feel that we come up short.

"I would venture that there is a strong tie between job dissatisfaction, on the one hand, and a disproportionate concern with offspring's success in sports, on the other," writes Dr. David Elkind. "Children thus became the symbols or carriers of their parents' frustrated competitiveness in the workplace."[9]

A psychologist who counsels many stressed-out children told me the story of a fifth grader named Sam who had been made to carry the burden of his father's recent bankruptcy. The child was a straight-A student, a good multisport athlete and an elected member of the student council. He was, as one teacher described him, a "super-talented kid." That talent had always been a source of pride to his parents. After his father was forced to declare bankruptcy, Sam noticed that satisfying his parents became harder and harder. Instead of encouraging Sam to develop his talents, they wanted him to be the best in every area and pushed him to participate in more activities so that he could shine.

The psychologist told me that "one day the kid just shut down and said, 'I'm not doing this anymore. Since my dad lost his job I feel like there is a huge weight on my back that's crushing me. I mean, it's hard enough for me to live my own life. I can't live his, too.'"

Sam's resistance to his parents' pressures caused a lot of arguments, which eventually led them to the psychologist's office. "I told the parents that Sam is a wonderful kid whether he's involved in all these activities or not. I suggested that if they cut back on a couple of these things, it was going to be better for him, it was going to be better for them, and ultimately it was going to reflect better on them, because they were very image-conscious parents. He was their only child, and because of their financial problems, they were looking to their son to burnish their own self-image."

When Sam's parents realized the pressure they were unwittingly putting on their son, they were more than willing to do what they needed to do to put him back on track. They cut back on his activities and, more importantly, began to praise Sam when he did well instead of taking his performance for granted and asking him to do even better. Within a short time, Sam again became a happy and enthusiastic child.

The pressure on children can be even more intense, and can start earlier, when parents wait until they are older to start a family. All the planning and procrastinating sometimes gives parents more time to think of their child as the reservoir of all their hopes and dreams. That problem is magnified because, in many cases, older prospective mothers know that their first child will likely be their only child.

Paul and Tina are typical of a growing number of professional couples. They married when they were in their thirties and spent a number of years climbing the corporate ladder and securing their financial futures. Tina's biological clock kept ticking all the while. When Paul was forty years old and Tina thirty-eight, the couple decided to have a baby. After a year of trying unsuccessfully to become pregnant, they resorted to in vitro fertilization. The procedure was very regimented; everything was specifically timed, from hormone shots to sperm collection to implantation. But in the end, the procedure worked. After four arduous attempts, Tina was finally pregnant.

Tina managed her pregnancy as she did her career. She was used to performing important tasks in the professional world; she looked at child rearing the same way. She read practically every popular book about pregnancy and child rearing, and the information gave her a sense of control. At thirty-seven weeks into her pregnancy, she gave birth to healthy twin daughters. Yet she immediately began to worry that something was wrong with her newborns because they were "premature." The books she had read said a normal pregnancy usually lasts forty weeks. Therefore, by her reckoning, her kids were born three weeks early. Despite her doctor's assurance that thirty-seven weeks is a normal, term pregnancy, Tina considered them premature and continued to worry about their well-being.

Tina quickly became overprotective. She kept careful records of the amount of urine and stool the children made; she also asked the pediatrician to weigh her children every day. She said she wanted to make sure they weren't falling "behind" other infants.

The pediatrician told me Tina's behavior is not at all unusual among older, professional parents. "Everything in their lives has been so premeditated, even the act of getting pregnant. Plus, they've waited so long to have a baby that they don't want to blow it. They become controlling and overprotective in an attempt to make sure their child turns out perfect. By recording her kids' urine, stool and weight, Tina was trying to exert control over their upbringing, using the only parameters that she could measure. Of course, it was all an illusion. She could no more control how much they went to the bathroom than she could their innate intelligence.

"Can you imagine using your child's urine output as a means of comparison with other children? Lord help those children when they get older!"

"Mini-Me"

One of the reasons to have children is to pass on our genes . . . to grasp some small piece of immortality. We call it reproduction, but having a child is not the same as making a Xerox copy of oneself.

Evolution has fashioned an ingenious method to ensure that every child is unique (except, of course, identical twins, triplets, etc.) and different from either of its parents. Each sperm and egg contains a different genetic pattern; when the two come together at the moment of conception, a genetically distinct entity is formed.

Our children are thus not simply little versions of ourselves. They may share our genes, but they are not our clones. They may look, sound and even act like we do. But they often have different preferences, abilities and aptitudes. Sometimes we forget that fact.

In the movie *Varsity Blues,* James Van Der Beek plays a character named John Moxon, the quarterback of a championship high school football team that is the pride of its small Southern town. When the team loses after the players spend the night carousing at a strip bar, John's father, who was a benchwarmer on the team when he was in high school, angrily confronts his son.

"You got the opportunity of a lifetime!" he yells, pointing his finger at John.

"Playing football at West Canaan is not the opportunity of a lifetime," John protests.

"Your attitude's wrong, your tone of voice is wrong. This is your opportunity. . . ."

"For you!" John shouts. "Playing football at West Canaan may have been the opportunity of your life. But I don't want your life."

Dr. Severe says parents live vicariously through their children because "they believe if their children are perfect apples, they're perfect too."[10] But people who live a frenetically paced, scheduled, stress-filled lifestyle ought to hope that when it comes to their children, the apple falls far from the tree.

Dr. Jim Loomis, manager of Child and Family Support Services at Connecticut Children's Medical Center, says that separating your life, hopes and desires from your childrens' can be hard to do. "They are a reflection of us. We work out a lot of left-over issues with our parents, usually through our kids. It makes it very loaded to say, 'Boy, I love my kid even though he's having trouble learning,' because the kid is a reflection of us. So instead we say, 'No, you've got to be perfect, or you've got to be good at this, or you've got to measure up.'"[11]

How many of us can honestly say we want our children to grow up to be different than we are? I bet not many of us. Seeing our children as Mini-Me, as the character Austin Powers so aptly named his miniature clone in the movie *The Spy Who Shagged Me,* is only natural. Of course, the "me" that we use is often an idealized vision of ourselves. Heck, it's not easy to admit that we are imperfect or that our lifestyle may be unhealthy. Even if we are aware of it, it's hard to change the way we live after all these years.

Mundane Mayhem

Much of the stress we face is such a part of our everyday lives that we take it for granted. Over the course of many years, we have learned to accommodate the curve balls that life throws our way. (Or at least we think we accommodate them. The rising incidence of stress-related illnesses among adults, like headache, heart disease, fibromyalgia, back pain, etc., provides evidence to the contrary). Our children's defense mechanisms against stressful situations have not yet fully developed. Thus, things we think are a part of normal life may, to our children, be extremely stressful.

Judsen Culbreth, editor-in-chief of *Scholastic Parent & Child* magazine, says, "Think about if you went to a new job every year and you had a new boss, new coworkers and new situations, new expectations and new job skills. It can be scary."[12]

According to one expert, the key component to stress is change. Consistency is important to a developing child. When life at home or school changes, uncertainty is introduced into the child's life. That uncertainty is often very stressful.

Family instability is one of the major causes of "mundane mayhem" in children's lives.[13] Whether it's the parents' relationship, the birth of a sibling or fighting with one you already have, or concerns about privacy or finances, anything that threatens the family's stability threatens the child's health. Nothing is more destabilizing than divorce.

Jacqueline was a happy, healthy child who did well in her suburban Boston area school. She and her professional parents lived what appeared to be a normal life, until her parents filed for divorce. Jacqueline was fifteen years old at the time, and the news of the breakup hit her hard, especially when she learned that her dad had decided to move to Arizona to "start his life over again."

After her dad left, Jacqueline's relationship with her mom deteriorated. They fought over the little things that mothers and teenage daughters often fight about: how much money to spend on clothing, a request for a second phone line, coed sleepovers. However, when her mother imposed (normal) curfews and restrictions on her daughter's social activities, Jacqueline rebelled. In a rage, she packed her bags and moved to Arizona to live with her father.

Jacqueline assumed her father would be more easygoing than her mother. Like most teenagers, she chafed at restrictions and hoped her father would let her do what she wanted. He did. The problem was that he didn't really care what Jacqueline did; he didn't pay much attention to her after she arrived in Arizona. He was trying to start over again, and it was obvious to Jacqueline that "starting over" meant severing his ties with his past, including his daughter.

Jacqueline was devastated. She spent the remainder of the summer in Arizona, then returned to Massachusetts. Shortly after she moved back home with her mother, Jacqueline developed frequent episodes of dizziness, nearly fainting on a number of occasions. A pediatrician, a neurologist and a cardiologist examined her but found nothing physically wrong. Eventually, all three physicians arrived at the same diagnosis: psychological stress, caused by her parents' divorce and subsequent rejection by her father. After months of therapy, Jacqueline's dizzy spells became less frequent, and her relationship with her mother began to improve.

Thirteen-year-old Stephanie has not been as lucky. She grew up watching her parents fight all the time. "There was never a time when my parents were just happy with each other," Stephanie said. "When they weren't yelling and screaming at each other, they were ignoring each other."

When their parents split up, Stephanie and her older brother were hardly surprised. However, neither child was prepared for the acrimony of divorce proceedings that followed. The custody battle was harsh and protracted, including charges and countercharges of incompetent parenting, infidelity and psychological abuse. Eventually, Stephanie's mother won custody of both kids, but the fighting didn't stop when the court case concluded. Stephanie's parents continued to fight on the phone and in person, when they saw each other at school functions or other occasions.

Stephanie bravely tried to stay neutral between her warring parents. However, the stress of the messy divorce became visible when Stephanie began to gain weight because of overeating. In the course of six months, Stephanie went from being a normal-sized teenage girl to an obese one. Her obesity became so severe that she was ostracized in school. Her pediatrician examined her and ran tests to make sure nothing was physically wrong. When the doctor concluded that Stephanie's weight gain was due to stress-induced overeating, he recommended psychological counseling.

One year later, Stephanie remains obese, stressed and ostracized in school. She sees a psychologist twice a week, but the root cause of her stress remains unchanged; her parents still fight with each other. Until that situation comes to some resolution, Stephanie's condition is unlikely to improve.

Headache is one of the more common illnesses children develop when poor family dynamics lead to what some doctors call "communication disorder," or poor communication between parents and children. One study looked at children whose doctors thought their migraines were related to troubled family dynamics. One group of children, along with their parents, received family therapy; the other group of children was treated with daily headache medication. Who did better? Neither, and that's the point. Family therapy that stressed parent-child communication worked just as well as drugs to treat a stress-related illness.[14] Which would you rather use to treat your child's headaches?

Relationships fail and marriages fall apart. Those occurrences are realities in our modern culture. Parents can't always control every situation, and our children have even less control than we do. They don't choose their parents, and they certainly don't choose to have their parents divorce. When divorce happens, we sometimes underestimate the impact it will have on our children; worse, we might use the children as pawns for our own selfish means. In either case, our children often pay a steep price for the choices we make in our lives.

". . . Spinning Wheel, Got to Go 'Round"

Another choice we make, consciously or subconsciously, is how much we let our own pressures divert us from being involved in our children's lives. I like to think of the family as functioning like a bicycle wheel. The family unit is at the center of the wheel, it is the hub to which a bicycle frame attaches. Shooting out from the family hub are many spokes, each of which represents a societal force that tries to pull us away from the hub. In our daily lives, many spokes tug at us, distract us and demand our attention: work (often for both parents), friends, leisure activities, financial pressures, chores, etc. In a bicycle wheel, the spokes only extend so far; they end at the point of attachment to the rim and the tire. In our lives, the centrifugal forces pulling us away from the family hub often work without restraint. We fail to place a protective rim around the family, or to say, "That's enough. It's now time for the family." Without a rim, a bicycle wheel cannot function. So we must find ways to place limits on the forces pulling at us from all sides. Each family may have a different-sized wheel; they may have spokes of different numbers and lengths. As long as the hub remains together, and we pay attention to our children, the bicycle will roll smoothly down life's various highways and byways.

Economic pressure is one of the biggest bumps we face on those roads. Two incomes are often necessary to pay for essentials like housing, groceries, child-care, transportation and clothing. Then, parents also have to worry about paying for family vacations, their children's education and their own retirement. This task is a challenge for most

American families, even those whom many people might consider "wealthy."

Of course, the "very wealthy" usually don't have these kinds of worries. For the rest of us, however, either staying afloat or moving up the economic ladder is a constant struggle. We make the task much harder by spending money as fast as we make it, forcing us to work harder and longer in order to earn more. This vicious cycle emerges from a combination of materialism, ambition and necessity.

The destructive effects of economic pressures on the family unit are nowhere more visible than in the neediest among us. Unstable family structures cause poverty,[15] but poverty itself can also rip families apart, damaging children in the process.

One school nurse who works in a poverty-stricken area in Pennsylvania says, "The area is also violent with a high incidence of crime and drug and alcohol abuse. The parents/guardians I work with are usually undereducated and stressed. It's difficult for many to cope due to early parenting and pressure now to work. Pennsylvania is strongly into welfare reform, so parents now must find work."[16] Those parents now have less time to spend with their kids. This nurse says many of these children turn to drugs, crime and gangs because of the financial pressures forcing their parents to spend increasing amounts of time away from home.

This nurse has seen similar problems on the other side of the tracks. "I have also worked in two very wealthy school systems. My own experience [in these communities is that] the pressures children feel is caused by the general disengagement of parents. It's all about realistic expectations and parents 'being available.'" She says the parents in these upwardly mobile communities were so involved with their own financial pursuits that they were constantly pulled away from their families.

I see these financial pressures at work in my own community. A significant percentage of the men commute to New York City for work. They leave their houses to catch the train before their children wake up in the morning and return home at night after their children are asleep. No, I'm not being sexist. In my community, many of the women are stay-at-home moms; but for women who commute to work, the routine is the same as the men's. These parents are basically "weekend dads and moms," which doesn't make them bad parents; many of them are loving and caring. Still, the pursuit of money propels them away from their children five out of seven days each week.

For some of these parents, working that hard and spending so much time away from their families in order to accumulate wealth is a choice; for others, it's a necessity. In either case, the less accessible we are to our children, the more likely they are to end up like the kids described by the school nurse from Pennsylvania.

Talk Is Cheap

Children need us to set limits on their behavior in order for them to learn right from wrong, good from bad. However, as our society coarsens, the boundaries between acceptable and unacceptable behavior become blurred. We may teach children one thing, but society shows them the opposite. We tell them children shouldn't have sex yet they see young teens in sexual situations on television and in the movies. We tell them violence is wrong yet they "battle" with different Pokémon characters. We tell them that the most important thing is to do their best yet they see that only high achievers receive accolades, even if their efforts don't match their abilities. We tell them that money isn't everything yet they see the materialism that pervades our society. We preach the importance of family and loyalty yet they see divorce destroying families all around them. These kinds of mixed messages create conflicts in a growing child's mind. Those conflicts cause confusion and stress.

Completely shielding our children from all the stressful forces they will encounter in their daily lives is impossible. The best we can do is limit their exposure to the most harmful influences and help them deal with the rest. This ongoing battle can make you feel like David fighting the societal Goliath. Just remember: David won that battle. So can you. You don't even have to invest in a slingshot.

The best way to help your child deal with the pressure around him is to talk about it. However, too many of us think that if we have a conversation about sex or violence or some other issue, we've done our parental duty. We feel better, relieved. After all, talking to your preteen about sex is not easy—but thinking that an isolated conversation can help your child stand up to the stresses of the world is a big mistake. The message doesn't get through unless it's repeated time and time again.

A Kaiser Family Foundation study confirms the need for repetition. In this study, many kids said their parents rarely talk to them about their problems. When they do, the conversations are "not very memorable." Half of the children between eight and eleven years old don't have any clue what their parents said to them. "These issues need to get talked about on an ongoing basis," says the Kaiser Family Foundation's Tina Hoff. "This isn't an issue where you have a big talk and you check this off your to-do list."[17] That concept is difficult for many of us. Talking to our children is not something that can just be "scheduled." Parenting is a full-time job that requires availability, flexibility and sensitivity. Here are ten tips to make that job easier.

1. Start early
2. Initiate conversations with your child . . .
3. . . . Even about sex and relationships
4. Create an open environment
5. Communicate your values
6. Listen to your child
7. Try to be honest
8. Be patient
9. Use everyday opportunities to talk
10. Talk about it again and again[18]

Talk is cheap and easy (once you get over the fear of broaching the topics of sex, drugs and rock 'n' roll!), and it's an effective way to give our children a sense of stability in an otherwise unstable world. If we can create an atmosphere in which they feel safe talking to us, we can learn what stresses them out and, hopefully, help them cope.

We can also try not to add to their stress. Life in an unstable world is hard enough without piling on unnecessary parental pressures. When we over-schedule our kids, set unrealistic expectations, instill a winner-take-all attitude or force them to grow up too quickly, we can shatter the sense of safety, security and stability within our homes. That can make them sick.

6757058862

READER/CUSTOMER CARE SURVEY

BA1

We care about your opinions. Please take a moment to fill out this Reader Survey card and mail it back to us.
As a special **"thank you"** we'll send you exciting news about interesting books and a valuable **Gift Certificate**

Please PRINT using ALL CAPITALS

First
Name [   ] MI.[ ]

Last
Name [   ]

Address [   ]

City [   ] ST [ ] Zip [   ]

Phone # ([_ _ _]) [_ _ _] - [_ _ _ _]   Fax # ([_ _ _]) [_ _ _] - [_ _ _ _]

Email [   ]

(1) Gender:
○ Female
○ Male

(2) Age:
○ 13-19   ○ 40-49
○ 20-29   ○ 50-59
○ 30-39   ○ 60+

(3) Your children's age(s):
Please fill in all that apply:
○ 6 or Under   ○ 15-18
○ 7-10   ○ 19+
○ 11-14   ○ 1   ○ 3
                ○ 2   ○ 4+

(8) Marital Status:
○ Married
○ Single
○ Divorced / Widowed

(9) Was this book:
○ Purchased For Yourself?
○ Received As a Gift?

(10)How many HCI books have you bought or read?

(11) Did this book meet your expectations?
○ Yes
○ No

(12) How did you find out about this book? *Please fill in ONE.*
○ Personal Recommendation
○ Store Display
○ TV/Radio Program
○ Bestseller List
○ Website
○ Advertisement/Article or Book
○ Catalog or Mailing
○ Other _____

(13) What FIVE subject areas do you enjoy reading about most? *Rank only FIVE.*
Choose 1 for your favorite, 2 for second favorite, etc.

	1	2	3	4	5
Self Development	○	○	○	○	○
Parenting	○	○	○	○	○
Spirituality/Inspiration	○	○	○	○	○
Family and Relationships	○	○	○	○	○
Health and Nutrition	○	○	○	○	○
Recovery	○	○	○	○	○
Business/Professional	○	○	○	○	○
Entertainment	○	○	○	○	○
Sports	○	○	○	○	○
Teen Issues	○	○	○	○	○
Pets	○	○	○	○	○

FOLD HERE

BA1

9396058864

(25) Are you:
○ A Parent?
○ A Grandparent

(18) Where do you purchase most of your books?
Please fill in your top TWO choices only.
○ General Bookstore
○ Religious Bookstore
○ Warehouse / Price Club
○ Discount or Other Retail Store
○ Website
○ Book Club / Mail Order

(20) What type(s) of magazines do you SUBSCRIBE to?
Fill in up to FIVE categories.
○ Parenting
○ Sports
○ Fashion
○ Business / Professional
○ World News / Current Events
○ General Entertainment
○ Homemaking, Cooking, Crafts
○ Women's Issues
○ Other (please specify) _____

Five

STRESS TEST

When most doctors say they want you to take a stress test, they want to hook you up to an EKG machine, put you on a treadmill and measure the function of your heart while you exercise.

I want you to take a stress test, too, but not one that involves an EKG or a treadmill. Instead, I want you to take a look at your child's life, critically evaluate it and determine whether the instability in her world is stressing her out. This stress test doesn't check your heart but instead requires you to take a gut check about the way you and your child live your lives.

Know Your Child

It's time for your five-year-old son to go to his karate class. You reach into his closet, take out his karate outfit and prepare to put it on him. Suddenly he says, "I don't want to go to karate." You ask why and he answers, "My stomach hurts and my body hurts all over." He says he likes karate, but for the second week in a row he hasn't felt well enough to go. Is he trying to tell you something? Is he becoming too stressed out from all his after-school activities?

A nine-year-old girl who is usually well behaved

suddenly starts fighting with her brother every day. Most of the fights are over little matters that would not normally cause a problem. Whenever her parents ask her what's going on, she ends up fighting with them, too. The girl's parents tell her they're upset and that her problem, whatever it is, better not keep her from making straight As again this year. Is the pressure to perform academically affecting this girl, or are her outbursts just a normal aspect of preadolescent behavior?

The only way to answer these questions is to know your child, which is the key to preventing burnout or at least to detecting the signs early enough that you can do something about it. If you know his or her limits, you will know when to say "enough is enough." Of course, figuring out what's going on inside your child's head is not always easy; unfortunately, children don't come with instruction manuals. Even if they did, each child is unique, so you would have to write a different manual for each one.

Children almost always give us signals when they feel stress or when they are in danger of burning out. Some signals are obvious; others are subtle. Dr. Sal Severe, author of the book, *How to Behave So Your Children Will, Too!* (Penguin Putnam 1997), says, "Kids are very good about showing those things; parents are not always good at seeing them. They want to overlook them or rationalize them. That's where we get into trouble."[1]

One way to make sure we don't overlook or rationalize these signs is to take an organized approach to monitoring our children. I often recommend parents follow a series of steps that I call COIN: conversation, observation, interpretation and negotiation.

Conversation: Talk to your child. Too often our lives

are so busy with work, social activities, errands, church groups, charity work, etc., that we forget to sit down and talk to our children. You can learn so much about what a child is feeling when you just let them talk.

Sometimes when we talk to children, we do it very superficially. If a child tells you something is wrong and your response is something like, "Don't worry. Everything will be fine," what you're telling her is that you don't really want to talk about her problems. According to Dr. Bettie Youngs, author of *Stress and Your Child,* when we utter those kinds of superficial statements, "We seek to momentarily soothe the child without fully understanding the anxieties underlying the pain he or she is feeling. When we aren't sensitive to the stress our children are experiencing, we forfeit the chance to help them learn healthy ways to handle such feelings as loss, powerlessness, fear, anger and hurt."[2]

Observation: Of course, conversation won't always work. Some children withdraw and turn inward in response to stress. Others are too young to fully express their feelings in words. But both groups of children can tell you they're stressed even when they can't, or won't, speak. They communicate through their behavior. The problem is that we often don't pay attention to their behavioral signals. Observation comes in handy here.

The five basic senses are sight, sound, touch, smell and taste. When we observe our kids for signs of stress, we need to use at least two of those senses, sight and sound, but a sixth sense, intuition, may be just as important. We should pay attention to our gut. If we feel something is wrong, we must take notice. That's what knowing your child is all about.

Interpretation: Talking to and watching our children

are not enough. Chances are good that children won't come out and tell you, "I'm burning out." Therefore, we have to interpret what we see or hear. The behavioral guidelines below will help you with this task.

Negotiation: Once you determine your child is showing signs of stress, you have to negotiate your way through all of the potential causes in your child's life. You may need to talk to your child for her opinion, keep a calendar of activities to chart how much "free time" your child has and record any physical complaints or sick days on the calendar. You may also want to discuss your concerns with your pediatrician; in some cases, you may need a child or family psychologist to help you find out the source of the situation.

Sending Out an S-O-S (Sign of Stress)

My mother once told me that my younger brother would always be her baby. He's thirty-seven years old now. Although he probably wouldn't appreciate the reminder, I understand what she means. Still, if my brother suddenly forgot his toilet training, even Mom would agree that her "baby" has a problem.

That example may be an exaggeration, but it demonstrates an important point. You have to consider your child's age when you try to decide if he or she is showing signs of stress. It's normal for a three-year-old to throw a crying, foot-stomping tantrum (as long as they don't do it regularly). However, they don't usually malinger, that is, they don't usually make up physical symptoms like headaches or stomachaches. On the other hand, a ten-year-old who is still throwing tantrums may be showing a sign of stress.

Children may show that they are stressed out in different ways, depending on their age. Still, common signs of stress exist among all children. In fact, you will see quite a bit of overlap of symptoms in the lists on the following pages. But experts say children in different age groups often have different symptoms when they are stressed out. The age categories are somewhat arbitrary and are simply intended as a guide to help you detect whether your child is sending you an S-O-S.

Toddlers: Ages Two to Five

Patty N. noticed something wrong with her four-year-old son, Josh, on one of those rare days when she tagged along on a play date. Josh had appeared tired after preschool and told his mother he wanted to go home. However, Patty wanted to stimulate and socialize Josh, so she drove him to his friend's house anyway.

At first it went smoothly. Josh and his friend played quietly, and they both seemed happy. Unfortunately, the tranquility lasted only fifteen minutes. Then Josh suffered a meltdown. On two separate occasions he broke into unprovoked temper tantrums. Finally, Patty had no choice but to take him home. She had seen this happen many times before. Josh frequently had tantrums during after-school play dates.

Patty worried. Something was wrong with her son, but she didn't see Josh's tantrums for what they were: an S-O-S. He was overscheduled and was exhibiting two classic signs of stress: exhaustion and emotional instability. In a toddler, up to the preschool age, look for:

- Hyperactivity
- Nervous habits, tics, excessive blinking, hair twirling, nail biting

- Constant fearfulness
- Tantrums
- Regression—for example, a child who is toilet trained suddenly starts going to the bathroom in his pants again
- Aggressive behavior
- Changes in sleep patterns
- Loss of appetite
- Loss of confidence
- "Clinginess," like a child who suddenly starts clinging to his parent's leg when he meets a new person or is in an unfamiliar situation
- Chronic diarrhea
- Belly pain
- Headaches
- Frequent colds and other minor illnesses

Even toddlers can have physical, psychological or behavioral symptoms when they are stressed. Unfortunately, they often can't or won't tell you what they are feeling. Direct questions about their feelings can seem threatening. Some experts suggest using inanimate objects like stuffed animals or dolls to explore a child's feelings. If you hold up the doll and ask your child how the doll is feeling, you may get your answer. A child might be less threatened projecting her feelings onto a doll than expressing them as her own.

Older Children: Ages Six to Twelve

At ten years old, Danny was the envy of most of his friends. He was a gifted athlete and seemed to excel at any sport he tried. He was the star pitcher on his Little League team and the leading scorer on his soccer and basketball teams. His father, who had also been a first-rate athlete, basked in the glory of his son's achievements.

Actually, Danny's dad did more than that. He pushed Danny to be the best, forcing him to practice after school, on weekends and on holidays. As Danny's skills improved, so did his father's expectations. If Danny pitched a one-hitter, his dad would focus on what went wrong with the pitch that was hit for a single. If he shot 80 percent from the free throw line, his dad would "encourage" him to practice his free throws.

Danny friends envied his talent. He was jealous of their freedom from expectations, scrutiny, parental disappointment and the fear of failure. When his friends kicked a soccer ball and missed the goal, it was no big deal. When Danny kicked it, he was supposed to score. One day Danny built up his courage and told his father he didn't want to play sports anymore. His father refused to let him quit.

Danny reluctantly continued to play, but he began to complain of vague muscle aches and pains in his arms and legs that grew worse as the season progressed. Doctors could find nothing physically wrong with him, but the pain continued. Eventually, the chronic pain forced Danny to the sidelines.

Danny is a classic example of how stress can affect an older child. The signs of stress in this age group are plentiful, and they include:

- Unexplained aches and pains
- Frequent illnesses
- Headaches
- Stomachaches
- Changes in sleep patterns
- Changes in eating patterns

- Nightmares
- Anxiety
- Nervous habits
- A drop in grades
- Lack of emotions (a so-called "flat affect")
- Refusal to go to school
- Outbursts of temper
- Low self-esteem
- No desire to be with friends

Children in this age group may tell you if they feel stressed out; they are certainly capable of expressing themselves. You should probably try a direct approach first, although some kids may not respond to it. Younger or less mature children may not even know why they feel or act the way they do.

If you think your child is sending out an S-O-S and you can't figure out why, Dr. Ray Guarendi, author of *You're a Better Parent Than You Think You Are,* suggests that you "Play twenty questions if you have to: 'How's that new teacher? Is that older girl still giving you a hard time?'"[3] Like toddlers who project their feelings onto dolls or stuffed animals, some older children may feel more comfortable expressing their feelings and frustrations through art. That some of us may need a child's drawing to tell us we're pushing them too hard is ironic indeed.

Adolescents: The Teenage Years

Adolescence is difficult enough: hormones rage, the opposite sex perplexes and popularity becomes ever so important. Those three factors alone are enough to stress out most teens. Parental pressure only adds to the problem. Someone recently told me about a girl named Mary. Her story is a good example of how stress can make a child sick.

At fifteen, Mary was like many girls her age. She liked boys, was involved in school activities and had her own group of friends. She was also an outstanding student: her grade point average (GPA) of A- was near the top of her class. Unfortunately, this GPA didn't satisfy her parents. They were both Ivy League–trained lawyers and had been pushing Mary to go to law school since she was in fourth grade.

Mary liked the idea of becoming a lawyer, and her GPA was certainly good enough to gain entrance into a good college. The problem was that she knew her parents would not be satisfied unless she attended an Ivy League school, just as they did. Mary didn't really care about the Ivy League, but she didn't want to disappoint her parents, so she tried as hard as she could to raise her GPA from an A- to an A.

The first time Mary suffered palpitations was while she was taking a final exam. She was having trouble answering a couple of the questions when she began to feel her heart racing. She tried to ignore the symptoms, but the more she struggled with her test, the worse her palpitations became. After a few minutes she started sweating and feeling lightheaded. Luckily, the teacher noticed that Mary didn't look well and immediately took her to the nurse's office. After an hour in the nurse's office, the symptoms disappeared. The next day, Mary was allowed to take a different, make-up exam; she earned an A.

Mary had more palpitations after that. On two occasions, she became sick while taking a test. Her parents took her to the doctor, who treated Mary with a medication called a beta-blocker to prevent palpitations. The medicine didn't do the job. The symptoms recurred whenever Mary had difficulty with an exam. An astute teacher recognized the pattern and recommended that Mary see the school psychologist, who saw right away that Mary's symptoms were caused by the pressure on her to be perfect.

The psychologist gave Mary's parents his diagnosis. They were indignant. They strongly reaffirmed their belief in setting high standards for their daughter and denied that her symptoms had anything to do with a fear of failure. They believed that Mary's problem was physical and that the answer was more medication.

I'm not sure whether Mary will eventually go to an Ivy League school, but her story is not unique. Doctors often misdiagnose teenagers with physical symptoms as having a medical condition when what they really have is a case of burnout.

Some of the symptoms or signs of a teenager on the verge of burnout are:

- Unexplained aches and pains
- Unexplained wheezing
- Headaches
- Stomachaches
- Changes in sleep patterns
- Changes in eating patterns, perhaps leading to anorexia or bulimia
- Anxiety
- Pounding or racing heart
- Chest pains
- A drop in grades
- Loss of concentration
- Anger
- Aggressive behavior

- Depression
- Low self-esteem
- Low energy level
- Emotional withdrawal from friends and family

Intense emotional stress can have a serious effect on children of all ages, especially adolescents. Suicide is the third leading cause of death for adolescents. Each year, almost a million American children either think about committing suicide or actually try to kill themselves.[4]

Of course, most children who feel intense pressure will never consider suicide. But children who are at risk usually send out an S-O-S, such as drastic changes in behavior, giving away possessions or suffering extreme depression. Many children will talk about suicide or make remarks about their lives being worthless or about their own deaths. Parents *cannot* ignore these warning signs. Children who attempt suicide feel desperate and are usually just crying out for help. We need to tune into those signals so we can help our children before they resort to desperate acts.

Suicide is the most drastic manifestation of stress. The other physical and emotional symptoms listed may not be as devastating, but they are dangerous in their own right. The effects of chronic stress, no matter the intensity, can be detrimental to our children's health and well-being.

Stress or Growing Pains?

If you've gone through the steps of conversation, observation, interpretation and negotiation, and you have identified physical or psychological signals that you think may be due to stress, then you have to ask yourself this question: "Are these behaviors really signs of stress or are they just normal growing pains?" You may have trouble telling the difference. Tantrums, anxiety, rebelliousness and physical ailments are all part of growing up. We may sometimes wish they weren't. In fact, those problems often cause us parents a lot of stress!

They are not, by themselves, signals that something is wrong in our child's life. Experts say you have to put them into context. There are some factors to consider when you try to figure out whether a behavior is normal or a sign of stress.

- **When will this end?** How many times have you asked yourself that question? The real question you should be asking yourself is this: is your kid just having a bad day, or are her bad days starting to outnumber her good ones? Isolated incidents are normal. A consistent pattern of incidents may be a sign that something is wrong.

- **A mountain or a molehill?** Take into account the intensity of your child's behavior. Tantrums, illnesses and arguments come and go, but once they pass, your child's life goes on as before. If, however, these issues become so severe that they interfere with your child's life, then they signal a problem. For example, a child having an occasional headache, stomachache or other illness is normal. When these complaints occur so frequently that he misses a lot of school, it is a good indication that something is wrong.

- **Dr. Jekyll or Mr. Hyde?** Everyone, even the youngest child, has his or her own range of behavior. Sometimes we call this behavioral range a person's temperament. Most parents instinctively know what their child's temperament is, including how he reacts to difficult situations, how he responds to people, etc. When the child's behavior changes or becomes inconsistent with his usual temperament, an underlying problem may be present.

In his normal state, Dr. Henry Jekyll would never have committed the monstrous acts of his alter ego, Mr. Edward Hyde. Children's behavior can also change when they are under chronic stress. When that happens, they may not act like monsters (hopefully!), but they certainly don't act like themselves, either. When children don't act like themselves, parents can search for a reason.

One way to tell whether your child's symptoms are normal growing pains or something worse is to chart the frequency and potential cause of the symptoms. As a headache specialist, I always ask my patients to chart their headaches, although it's not always easy. Many doctors ask their patients to chart various symptoms, but they either don't give the patient any guidance on how to do it, or they give them a chart that is so complicated that you'd need a Ph.D. to complete it.

With that in mind, I have developed a relatively simple way to chart your child's symptoms. You do not need any special paper or form; you can use your own calendar, date book or personal digital assistant. I like to divide the signs and symptoms of stress into three categories: physical, emotional and behavioral. All you have to do is write those words on each calendar day, leaving a space under each. Then, if your child displays a sign of stress, place a check mark next to the proper category, i.e., physical, emotional or behavioral. In the space below, log the symptom or sign of stress and what you think triggered it. For example:

Monday, December 3
✓ Physical
wheezing—got a C on his report card

Emotional

Behavioral

Keeping a log like this may help you determine whether you are right to worry about your child's behavioral or physical problems. You can instantly see the frequency and type of symptoms your child suffers. You may not always be correct about what causes the symptoms, but a log like this will help you identify the problem in the first place, and that is the most important thing you can do. The log will also be an enormous help to your child's doctor.

The Stress Test

No book can tell you whether your child is suffering from stress. However, you can use the following questions as a quick test to help you decide. Just check the phrases that apply to your child.
Does your child . . .

- behave differently than normal?
- miss a lot of school?
- seem emotionally withdrawn?

- have a lot of physical complaints?
- frequently become sick?
- do worse in school than he used to?
- avoid other children?
- seem angry?
- have frequent tantrums?
- complain about activities?
- refuse to participate in an activity he used to enjoy?

If you wrote a check mark next to any of these statements, your child may be stressed out. Take a break from your hectic life to look, listen and feel for an S-O-S. As one character said in the movie *The Matrix,* "The truth is out there." Your job is to find it . . . and then to do something about it.

Six

Too Much Time in the Backseat Instead of the Backyard

All work and no play makes Jack a dull boy.

Author Unknown

I t was a cold January night, yet the parking lot at Staples High School in Westport, Connecticut, was teeming with BMWs, luxury minivans and expensive sport utility vehicles. The turnout was unusually large for a Westport Board of Education meeting. The issue was how many hours a day should a child spend in kindergarten. The blustery New England weather wasn't going to keep parents from having their say on the subject.

Kindergarten in Westport traditionally followed an extended-day schedule. Children attended school from 8:30 A.M. to 1:15 P.M. every day, or slightly less than twenty-four hours a week. Now, however, the Board of Education was proposing to make kindergarten a full-day program. They wanted to add two hours a day, ten hours a week, ostensibly to provide more time for "individualized instruction and assessment," as well as to make room for newly mandated Spanish instruction.

Many people assumed parents would be thrilled. Westport is, in many ways, a typical upper-middle-class American community. Family, sports, education and intellectual stimulation are all valued as means of achieving success. Westport parents, like those in thousands of other towns across the country, do everything they can to give their children every possible opportunity to succeed. More is often equated with better.

So, surprisingly, of the approximately two hundred parents attending the meeting, roughly 95 percent of them came to register their opposition to extending the kindergarten day. Sitting in the audience, my first incredulous reaction was "What's going on here?"

One by one, the parents—one father, the rest mothers in their early thirties to mid-forties—lined up before the microphone to speak to the assembled board members and school administrators. Some of the speakers had prepared remarks, others spoke extemporaneously; some were emotional, others cool and rational; some were long-winded, others brief and to the point. But most of them had a similar message to deliver to their elected representatives: Don't extend the kindergarten day.

"[Instead of going to school those extra hours], we'd like them to be able to share their experiences with us before their older siblings arrive home from school. We'd like them to be able to play with their friends at home, to go on an occasional activity that they happen to enjoy, or to simply hang out, daydream and just be kids," said Nancy Yeats, whose third child was scheduled to attend kindergarten in the fall.

"We need to spend more time in discussion with our children at home. There's not enough time with our children, conversing over a good book or talking about what occurred at school," said Barbara Jackaloff.

"I don't think children should be institutionalized all day long," cried Jo Greenberg.

"There's too much overscheduling of our children," many of the parents said. I never thought I'd hear Westporters complain about their children having too many activities. These same parents enroll their young children in Scores Learning Centers to help them get into an Ivy League school a dozen years before they apply. They enroll their four-year-olds in soccer leagues; they hire individual baseball coaches so their kids can be jocks; they consider their preschoolers behind if they're not yet reading; and they put their kids in art classes in the hope that they'll be the next Picasso.

But then I asked myself a question: would Nancy really allow her children to "hang out" if they weren't in school those extra hours? Or would she fill their time with other structured activities?

Lisa Lebow was another parent who came to the meeting upset about the full-day kindergarten proposal. Her testimony was especially revealing: "All the wonderful programs I moved here for," she said passionately, "I now have to cram in on Saturday. I don't want to do that. I want to be with my children. . . . Let's let the kids be kids. Let's let them relax, let them have play dates, let them have music, art, swimming, all the things [the schools] can't provide in a one-on-one situation."

Lisa and her fellow parents' objections made a powerful impact on the board of education. The next week, the board bowed to the parental pressure and quashed the full-day kindergarten proposal. But despite their good intentions, it's likely that many of the parents who spoke against full-day kindergarten will "take advantage of the extra hours" by doing exactly what Lisa spoke about: shuttling their children back and forth between play dates, music, art classes, swimming and other activities. They will simply substitute personal overscheduling for what they perceived as institutional overscheduling.

Parents have become obsessed with keeping their kids busy. Manufacturers have caught on, too. They've produced Pop Tarts on a Stick for children on the go. I've even heard of a Baby Filofax to help organize children's daily schedule of activities. Let's face it, we're running our children ragged in the attempt to make them superchildren. If an hour goes by when they're not scheduled to participate in some activity, many parents view that hour as a nonproductive hole in the child's schedule.

Nine-year-old Melanie Polk, who lived only a couple miles away from the cafeteria in which the Westport Board of Education meeting took place, was a perfect example: school during the day, piano lessons twice a week, gymnastics and ballet classes, and French lessons. On the rare occasions Melanie was at home in the early evening, her parents often prodded her to practice the piano.

Melanie's schedule was neither unusual nor extreme when compared to others'. In fact, her life resembled that of thousands of children across the country who are supposedly on the fast track to success. To the outside observer, Melanie seemed like a happy, if ambitious, child. On the inside, however, stress was taking its toll. Eventually, the pressure broke through. Melanie began to complain of stomachaches and "feeling tired all the time." After two weeks, her mom took her to the doctor.

After examining Melanie and talking with her, Dr. Peter Czuczka, her pediatrician, immediately knew the diagnosis.

"I told her mom I thought her problems were

caused by the stress of running around, trying to do too much. She was only nine years old, for God's sake, yet her schedule was more packed than mine, and I work for a living," he said.

Melanie's mother was unconvinced.

"She's never complained to me before," she told Dr. Czuczka. "She loves her activities. No, I know there's something wrong with her . . . Lyme disease, maybe, or chronic fatigue syndrome."

"So I did the tests to reassure the mother," Dr. Czuczka continued, "but I knew they'd be negative. A quarter of my practice is made up of psychosomatic complaints, and a lot of that is from parents overscheduling their children."

Within days of cutting back on her scheduled activities, Melanie's stomachaches stopped and her energy level improved. Dr. Czuczka says recovery often takes less time than that.

"I often see their symptoms go away the minute their parents agree to cut back [activities]. It's scary."

Like so many other American children, Melanie was burned out, yet she was lucky. Her doctor recognized the real cause of her symptoms early, and her parents took the appropriate steps to relieve her schedule.

In their book *The 7 Worst Things Good Parents Do,* psychologists John and Linda Friel place "Push your child into too many activities" third on their list of destructive parenting practices. Their thesis is particularly appropriate with regard to overscheduling: "You can push your kids until they drop, and then push them a lot more, but the only thing you will produce are miserable adults who may become moderately successful in their careers, if they are lucky."

Of course, overscheduling is not a problem limited to Westport, Connecticut. From New York to Naples, Florida, in Kentucky and Kalamazoo, Missouri and Montana, and Texas and Tennessee, the age of instantaneous communication has connected us not only through commerce but also through competition.

Overscheduling is an insidious process that creeps up on you. Our lives in the rat race bleed over into the way we raise our children. We start them on the mouse mill at an early age.

I found out about this the hard way. When my son, Jacob, was four years old, he went to preschool five days a week, with two of those days being extended. He was also enrolled in karate classes and a Tumblebugs gymnastics program, and he often had a couple of play dates scheduled in the afternoon.

Jacob seemed to be tolerating this schedule well. He was happy, active and well adjusted. However, on many weekend days Jacob told us, "I just want to stay home and play with my toys," or "I don't want to go anywhere this weekend." Like many modern families, staying home wasn't always an option for our family. We had chores and errands, birthday parties to go to and social engagements to attend. Because of our hectic lifestyle, the only time to do many of these things was during the weekend. So we did what many parents do: we pushed Jacob to keep up with our pace.

Eventually, as Jacob continued to complain each weekend, we realized what he was trying, in his four-year-old way, to say: he was feeling overscheduled and needed to slow down, to shift his life into a lower gear. Once we did so, by setting up fewer play dates, letting him choose which activities he was involved in, running around less on the weekends

and making sure he had more "unstructured" play-
time each day, Jacob's complaining markedly
diminished.

Squeeze Play

Many of us are guilty of what I call productivity-
scheduling, or "efficiency parenting": the attempt to
direct every minute of a child's day toward some
predetermined goal. Pam Koner-Carrano, who runs
the Homework Club in Hastings-on-Hudson, New
York, has summarized this concept well: "For adults,
a day is only as good as how much we've gotten
done. Some people look at their kids' schedules the
same way."[1]
Unfortunately, the result is that those expensive
back yard swing sets found across suburbia often sit
silently, monuments to childhood lost.
Whatever happened to digging a hole in the back
yard until you reached water? Catching lizards?
Playing hopscotch or jumping rope with a neighbor?
Throwing a tennis ball one hundred times against
the garage door? Pretending you're Michael Jordan
(or in my case, Jerry West), dribbling the ball with
the clock ticking down, the crowd waiting for you to
sink the game-winning shot? Being a kid and enjoying your free time seems like an art lost to the overscheduled children of today.
Times have changed, however, and so have some of
the necessities of parenting. We used to know most of
our neighbors; now, even our next-door neighbors
may be total strangers. Our parents used to let us
ride our bikes to the local park or playground without
worrying about our safety; now we have to worry

about our children's faces ending up on the side of a milk carton. We used to be able to count on one of our parents, usually our mother, being home for us whenever we needed them; now, many families require that both parents work in order to make a living.

For precisely these reasons, structured activities are needed in today's society. They help ensure children's safety and provide adult supervision in a world in which we are increasingly disconnected from our neighbors and geographically dislocated from grandparents and our extended families. We can't go back to the way things were, but it's not too late to improve the way things are now.

Alvin Rosenfeld and Nicole Wise wrote in their book *Hyper-Parenting* (St. Martin's, 2000): "A generation or two ago, childhood was merely a journey along the way to adulthood. Like time spent traveling in a car, everyone understood that being a child would sometimes be dull and boring, at least from the adult's perspective. But children could be counted on to figure out how to pass their time along the way . . . sleeping, daydreaming, playing games, or just watching the world go by outside the window. Kids had to be creative because it was up to them to entertain themselves."

I am not trying to romanticize the past. No childhood is perfect, and certainly many opportunities available today would have made our childhood experiences richer and more stimulating. But programming every hour of our childrens' days has consequences.

Free time is slowly slipping away. In 1981, a little more than half a child's day was considered structured. Forty percent of it was free time. Since then, however, our children's schedules have become more and more structured. In 1998, according to a study conducted by the University of Michigan's Institute for Social Research, the amount of free time our children had each day had dropped to only 30 percent.[2] The bottom line: they're spending an increasing amount of time in the backseat instead of in the backyard.

Kelly, a mother of three who lives in a Houston suburb, says, "So many of my friends constantly run their children to soccer or softball practice, music lessons, karate, gymnastics, you name it! I chuckle at my friends who seem to enjoy all the busy-ness, while I find myself trying to understand why they do it."

Sociologist Sandra Hofferth, one of the authors of the University of Michigan study, says one reason for the decrease in free time is the rise in dual-career families. Children tend to have more time for free play when one parent stays home. But even stay-at-home parents are moving away from spontaneous outdoor activities to more structured ones. The reason is that other neighborhood kids are increasingly unavailable because they themselves are participating in structured activities.

This phenomenon is mostly one of the middle to upper classes. According to a University of California-Berkeley study, urban children from lower socioeconomic conditions rarely have the same recreational options—people, places and physical resources—available to them that middle- and upper-socioeconomic-class children have.

Clearly, advantages exist to having all those classes, museums, athletic leagues, tutors and coaches in your neighborhood. A middle ground is present between an overwhelming, high-pressure schedule of activities and recreational deprivation.

However, many of us have not yet found that middle ground, and a lot of us aren't even trying.

You don't need statistics to identify the problem. All you have to do is look inside the waiting rooms of pediatricians' and child psychologists' offices around the country. They are filled with children who are unable to decompress, too young to develop effective coping skills, and who have ended up with the chronic physical, psychological and behavioral symptoms of burnout.

Consider a child like Diane, a bright nine-year-old from the Midwest. Her well-intentioned parents pushed her hard to succeed. In a typical week, Diane had ballet, ice skating, gymnastics and piano lessons. When she wasn't in school, in the car or at an activity, she was often with a language tutor to make sure she stayed ahead of her classmates. According to a family friend, "Diane never gets a moment to play."

The stress finally caught up with Diane when she fainted during a family vacation. Her doctors found nothing wrong with her, but that fainting episode was only the beginning. Two months later, Diane started complaining of pain in her right leg that became so bad she had trouble walking. A pediatrician, two orthopedic surgeons and a Lyme disease specialist were unable to find anything physically wrong with her. Despite that, Diane walked with the aid of crutches for months and was unable to continue most of her extracurricular activities.

When Diane's leg pain finally went away, her parents encouraged her to restart her activities. She did, but soon afterward began to experience strange chest pains. Again, her doctors gave her a clean bill of health. That didn't stop the chest pains; they continue to this day.

Diane's story is a tragedy. Neither her parents nor her doctors have considered the possibility that her stressful schedule could be causing her symptoms. As a result, Diane is probably on her way to becoming a prepubescent burnout.

For some of these children, frighteningly, the worst is yet to come. Overscheduling may become dangerous as these children grow older. A new study shows that, on average, teenagers are getting about two hours less sleep at night than they need, putting them at risk for, among other things, automobile accidents, falling asleep in class and general moodiness.

"We want our kids to do more and more," says Dr. Mark Mahowald, director of the Minnesota Regional Sleep Disorders Center at Hennepin County Medical Center in Minneapolis. "We don't want them to give up anything that they are currently doing, so we have them take it off their sleep period."[3]

Play as Work

You have a job. I have a job. So do our children. Their job is to learn, explore, experience and develop. The way they do that is through play. If we don't work, we quickly become impoverished. Similarly, if children aren't allowed time for their work, which is playing, their childhood is the poorer for it.

"I think it's criminal. There's no reason for a child to take any kind of lesson before age six or seven," says Dr. David Elkind, whose landmark bestselling book, *The Hurried Child,* warned twenty years ago about the dangers of forcing kids to grow up too fast.[4] His advice may be a little too draconian. Some young children enjoy a ballet or a soccer game each week. However, overloading a child's schedule may, indeed, be harmful.

Sleep, rest, free time and play time are essential for children of all ages to decompress and cope with life's normal stresses. More than that, and especially for our youngest children, unstructured play time is how they learn, experience and develop. Play time empowers them to explore the world around them and teaches them to solve problems by themselves. Play helps them develop social and language skills and fosters emotional growth. Some studies show that children who are allowed to play are more creative and interact better with other children. Children who play are better at dealing with stress. Research also shows that children learn better when they have periods of rest and relaxation. "Cramming lots of activities doesn't get them further ahead," says Dr. Donald Freedheim, director of the Schubert Center for Child Development at Case Western Reserve in Cleveland.[5] Thus, the very purpose for overscheduling, creating a superchild, is self-defeating.

Despite evidence supporting the importance of free and unstructured play, too many of today's goal-oriented parents equate free time with wasted time. However, by scheduling more structured, "productive" activities at the expense of free play, parents may be thwarting the very goals their overscheduling is designed to ensure.

Get 'Em off the Mouse Mill as Quickly as You Can

There are two times I feel stress—day and night.

—Anonymous

I have this recurring fantasy. In the middle of every weekday, I disconnect from the Internet, shut down my computer, take the phone off the hook, set the beeper to silent, turn off my cell phone, push the mute button on the television and just hang out for a couple of hours. I never do it, of course. I'm as much a victim of our hyper lifestyle as the next person.

However, the important fact is that I *could* slow down and take a daily siesta if I really desired it. I have control over my schedule (within the limits of my job, family responsibilities, etc.); our children have little or no control over theirs, which may be the crux of the burnout problem.

In 1967, a researcher at the University of Pennsylvania performed an experiment in which he exposed dogs to uncontrollable shocks. He then put the dogs in a different cage where they could avoid the shocks simply by moving to a different part of the cage. What the researcher found was surprising: the dogs did not move to the safe area of the cage, despite receiving painful shocks while standing in the danger zone. The dogs had become conditioned to think that they could never escape the painful shocks, no matter what they did. Psychologists call this behavior "learned helplessness."

Kids are not dogs, of course (although sometimes we might wish that they were, so that when we say, "Sit, stay," they would obey). But overscheduled children may also suffer from learned helplessness because they have no control over their lives. As we run them ragged, we expose them to increased amounts of unavoidable stress, the psychological equivalent of shocking them. The stress of learned helplessness can result in the physical and psychological ailments often seen in burnout.

Learned helplessness is avoidable. So is burnout. You don't have to live your life in the fast lane, and neither does your child. All you have to do to keep from overloading your child is follow a few simple rules.

Get 'Em Out of the Backseat and into the Backyard

Stop the engine. Open the car door. Unbuckle your child's car seat and get her the heck out of there. She's not going to fall behind, lose out on an Ivy League scholarship or fail to make the Olympic team if she slows down for a few minutes. I promise.

Make some time every day for your child to be alone. Some parents worry that their child will become bored. But if they're never allowed to do nothing, they won't have a chance to use their imagination, to climb a tree, to daydream, to explore the world around them, even if it's only within the confines of their own backyard.

The unstructured time is important because it allows kids to recuperate from the more structured part of their day. Kids need to recharge their batteries, the same way a vigorous workout, a hot tub or a massage can help adults. Actually, the workout analogy is more appropriate than you may think. According to Dr. Dan Rees, a family therapist and associate professor in the social work department at Western Maryland College, free time exercises a different part of childrens' brains than when they're participating in an organized activity, allowing them to process what they've learned during structured activities and while socializing. They become more self-reliant, learning how to entertain themselves and think creatively. The result is that kids who spend time doing "nothing" may end up ahead of their overscheduled peers in the long run.[6]

Some experts suggest setting limits on the number of activities a child should participate in, depending upon their age.[7]

Age	Activity
Birth to three years	One activity once or twice a week
Four to six years	A couple of "low-pressure" activities are fine, but limit them to no more than three hours a week
Seven to nine years	Let them choose a maximum of two activities to participate in each week
Ten to twelve years	Limit your child to three activities

These limits should only be used as guidelines. Some children can handle more, some less. But just because they *can* handle more activities doesn't mean you *should* enroll them in more. One parent I've spoken to understands this well: "My son has been involved in basketball, baseball and karate, though not at the same time. The rule in our house is that he can choose one activity and cannot start another until the current one is completely finished. That's how we avoid the burnout of too many activities."

Another woman wrote to tell me that she felt comfortable enrolling her three-and-one-half-year-old daughter in ice skating and karate classes, but that was the limit: "She asks me to take her to dancing classes, but I'm holding back on that until at least next year. Basically, we want to keep the number of activities that require her to attend classes to two. For now, she has to make do with turning the music on and dancing around the living room with me."

A mother who lives in a rural community says that one of the advantages of where she lives is that she rarely sees children who are stressed out from over-scheduling: "If parents want any type of enrichment for their children—music lessons, dance, ice hockey, etc.—they have to drive sixty-five miles to the nearest town! For most parents, this just isn't possible. Not only can they not afford it, they don't have the free time from work to make it possible to drive so far on a regular basis.

"So, I guess if you live in a rural community and have parents of average means, you may be spared from the stress of overscheduling! Personally, I think it is great that the children have time to play after school (until they are old enough to have homework), to just hang around in the yard and swing and bike and climb trees and play with dogs."

She adds that she also wants her children to see museums, zoos, and other cultural and educational attractions, so she will drive sixty-five miles to the next town, "but not on a weekly basis."

Slow and Steady Wins the Race

Almost all of us are familiar with the story of the tortoise and the hare, yet when it comes to our own lives, we act like hares on amphetamines, hopping back and forth as if we're trying desperately to avoid becoming just another rabbit's foot dangling from a key chain.

The only reason you hear about overnight success stories is that they are so rare. Most of the time, slow and steady really *does* win the race. The same goes for your child's schedule. If you start slow and steady, you'll likely end up with the result you desire: a happy, stimulated, healthy, well-rounded child.

I remember the first time I went to a sushi bar. I had no idea what, if anything, I would like, so I was hesitant to place my order. Then my more experienced sushi-eating friends recommended a solution: order small amounts of a number of different things so that I could try a variety of dishes until I found one (or more) I liked. A local brewery near my house has the same philosophy. Instead of ordering a pint of beer, you can order a "taster," which consists of relatively small amounts of the various beers brewed on site. If you don't like the dark lager, you can always move on to the raspberry-flavored beer.

Sampling foods or beers or anything new in this fashion is something many people take for granted. We shouldn't. If such an approach works for us, it can work for our kids, too. Let them sample different activities and programs before committing to them on a regular basis. The more things they experience, the better they'll be able to determine which ones they really like and which they could do without. Make sure, however, not to overwhelm them with too much variety.

Variety may not be as important for toddlers as the amount of time spent doing the activity. With these young children, treating them like a tortoise is especially beneficial. For example, start your toddler with an activity that lasts only twenty or thirty minutes. If he turns cranky, cut back the time of the activity until he can handle it comfortably. Over time, he will be able to handle more activities without feeling stressed out.

Empower Your Child

Empowerment works best, of course, if your child is old enough to clearly express her feelings, but may be applicable even with relatively young children. Explain the proposed activity and the time commitment required, then ask her if she wants to do it. This approach will give her a sense of control over her life and will give you some important feedback about her state of mind. Empowerment is a great way to avoid the pitfall of learned helplessness.

Some children will undoubtedly say they want to do everything. And why not? Their friends do it; their parents do it. It's only natural that they would want to keep up with everyone else's pace. Our job as parents is to make sure they don't. A hyperactive pace is one aspect of our lives we shouldn't want them to inherit from us. One way to do that, while still empowering our children, is to limit the number of activities they can participate in, but leave the choice of which activities up to them. One California mother came up with a perfect solution: she told her six-year-old daughter she could participate in two organized activities a week, then presented her with a list of eight to choose from. The little girl chose ballet classes and piano lessons; her mother now says her daughter has been less cranky and has had more energy since she assumed some measure of control over her own schedule.

Provide a Day of Rest

Even God rested after six straight days of hard work. Some religions have codified this day of rest as part of their laws and traditions, not only because the Bible says so, but also because we need the break. These religions have long recognized the importance of time for rest, reflection and family interaction.

Of course, you don't have to be religious to incorporate a day, or even just a couple of afternoons or evenings, of rest into your family's busy schedule. Setting aside one day each weekend to just hang out with the family would help children (and adults) decompress from their busy week.

A woman named Amber is on the right track. She e-mailed me: "It's Saturday morning. We're at home for the whole day. Right now my child is running Hot Wheels through a wrapping-paper tube track, and a few minutes ago he was painting with watercolors. All things he wants to do. Our whole day is not choreographed. He can start and finish when he wants to. He can take a break and look at a book or watch *Rugrats,* or he can color, a totally unstructured day. It's my belief that that's more important than having every minute of your life scheduled. Tomorrow we will have soccer after Sunday school, then we will take the rest of the day easy, too."

Encouraging families to spend more downtime is the goal of one group of parents in a suburb of Minneapolis, Minnesota. They have formed a group called "Family Life 1st!" whose goal is to stop what some experts call scheduled hyperactivity and reclaim time for the family.[8] They have come up with the concept of a seal of approval that they plan to bestow upon organizations and activities that are family friendly.

Another community that is rebelling against over-scheduling is Arcadia, Indiana. One of their schools, Hamilton Heights Middle School, has started giving students Homework Break coupons for one week a year if they spend time doing something with their family.[9] Many Arcadia parents have thanked the school principal for recognizing that family time should be just as important as homework in the lives of middle school children. As Dr. John Friel told me, "When children and parents don't have the time to connect emotionally . . . you wind up with some pretty serious psychological problems."

Take the Whole Family's Schedule into Account

Marks's First Law of Parenting states that the more children you have, the more time you'll have to spend hauling them back and forth to their respective activities. A corollary to that is Marks's Second Law of Parenting, which states that the more time you spend in the car shuttling between activities, the less quality time you spend with your child—unless, of course, you define quality time as listening to your children complain, scream in the backseat, talk incessantly (while you're too distracted to respond) and ask, "Are we there yet?" every five minutes.

I would imagine that few people became parents so they could be transformed into chauffeurs. As one mother of three told me, "I do not believe it is my job to live in the car, running kids here and there." Unfortunately, that's what often ends up happening when we pack our children's schedules with too many extracurricular activities.

Take the whole family's schedule into account when you sign your children up for activities. If not, you may end up robbing Peter of your time to pay Paul, and everyone gets gypped in the process. Remember, if you're stressed out from all of their activities, chances are your children are stressed out, too.

One mother told me her secret to dealing with her family's hectic schedule: "As a busy mother with four children, my husband and I were, and still are, protective of our family time and sanity. During the school year each child was allowed one activity outside of the normal busyness that school presents. If they chose ballet or music lessons, etc., they had to make a one-year commitment to stick with it. In the summertime, we did allow more latitude.

"This has allowed me some sanity in my driving routines. I feel one of the most important rituals we have is family dinner at six o'clock each evening. It has gotten harder as the kids get older, but they all know and respect this time together."

Meals Should Be Served on a Table, Not on a Dashboard

Does this sound familiar? It's 5:30 P.M., and you've been shuttling your child back and forth between school and extracurricular programs for most of the afternoon. You're tired. Your child's tired. Everyone's getting hungry. But basketball practice starts in an hour. There's not enough time to go home and make something for dinner; besides, you're too tired to even think about cooking. As you drive down the street, you see your favorite fast-food restaurant. You know you shouldn't, but what choice do you have? So you enter the drive-through lane and pick up something quick, which you and your son eat while you continue to your next destination.

Not exactly quality time with your child. Still, the scenario is familiar to most of us and is emblematic of our hurried lifestyles. Sometimes dashboard dinners can't be avoided. If, however, a large percentage of your child's meals are eaten on the run, that's a pretty good indication he's been overscheduled.

Suggesting that every family eat dinner together every night would be an ideal concept, if a bit Pollyanna-ish. That goal would place a de facto limit on the number of activities that could be scheduled after school (unless the family didn't meet for dinner until late at night). But if nightly dinners aren't realistic for today's hurried families, at least parents can try to set aside two or three nights a week for the entire family to sit around the table together. This structure would serve as a brake and help slow the pace of their children's lives, while also providing quality time for parents and children. Such quality time is the factor that has been most consistently associated with a child's success later in life. Thus, by slowing down, parents would actually be doing more for their children than rushing them from one activity to another.

A recent study backs this up. It found that adolescents who ate fewer than five meals a week with their parents were more likely to have anxiety, depression or other mental health problems than those who shared at least six meals a week with their parents.[10] The researchers concluded that sharing daily meals with the family represents an important "union ritual" that promotes adolescent mental health.[11]

One mother I know has come up with a novel idea to ensure that her family spends time together. Because of her husband's work schedule, the whole family found eating dinner together during the week impossible. Instead, she started a practice that she calls "fruit chat." She feeds her children early in the evening. When her husband comes home, the parents eat dinner and the children eat fruit with them. Although the whole family is not eating dinner at the same time, they're still sitting at the table together, spending time with each other and talking about the day before the children go to bed. The children look forward to fruit chat each night as a chance to laugh, share, bond and decompress with their parents and siblings.

Don't Substitute TV Time for Downtime

Moderate amounts of television will not bring down civilization, nor will it turn children into mind-numbed robots. Too much TV, however, may be harmful. There's evidence that watching too much television can pose a health risk by making our children more sedentary, and television violence may even lead them to behave more violently.[12]

However, at some times, watching TV may be helpful in winding children down after a long day. You should probably set limits, though, on how long your child watches television or plays video games. One mother of three in Houston, Texas, says that her children benefit from a little time to zone out in front of the TV at the end of a busy day. She allows them to watch television for one hour a day, as long as the show is nonviolent. When the hour is up, she turns off the TV and tells them to find other things to do. She says the children play together with renewed energy and enthusiasm after their hour of passive relaxation.

Some children who aren't used to having unstructured time have trouble figuring out what to do with it. Eventually, however, they will learn to find their own activities, use their imagination and play with their siblings. They will learn to deal with boredom. The down time will help them grow both intellectually and emotionally.

SEVEN

MAKING SOUFFLÉS

Children are a little like dessert soufflés. To make a soufflé, you have to mix all the ingredients in the proper proportions, mold it into the right shape and cook it for precisely the right amount of time. When it is ready, the soufflé is gorgeous and delicious. However, if you don't cook it long enough, the ingredients don't have the chance to rise properly; the soufflé wilts, the dessert is ruined. The same is true, to some extent, for children. All the ingredients are there, they just have to be "cooked" properly so the children can develop and rise to their potential.

Marc is one example. He was a three-year-old boy who was acting out at home, was always hyper and seemed to be bouncing off the walls. He didn't listen to his parents and threw temper tantrums without much provocation. Frustrated and exhausted, Marc's parents took him to the pediatrician with the hope that he could save their son.

After a few questions about Marc's physical condition, the doctor asked the parents about Marc's daily schedule, which consisted of day care from 8:00 A.M. to 4:00 P.M., followed on some days by ice hockey classes and, on others, karate classes. His dad said he enrolled Marc in these classes because he thought they might "curb his energy and help him excel."

As the parents were speaking, Marc began to bang on the exam table with a toy. Without moving from his chair, his dad said, "Marc, please stop banging. That's not appropriate here. Please stop." Marc ignored him, and his dad repeated himself, this time in a harsher tone of voice. "Marc. Stop banging right now!" Marc continued to ignore him. At that point, the pediatrician stood and approached the child. Bending down, he took Marc's hands in his own and looked into the child's eyes. The doctor said, "Marc, do you want to show me that toy truck?" Marc gleamed and proudly showed his doctor the toy. After a few moments, the doctor turned to the parents and said, "You are good parents, and you have a normal, healthy three-year-old son. My advice to you is: worry less about pushing him to excel and more about playing with him. There is too much structure here. Play with your son. Be with him. You will notice a difference."

Is This How to Build a Brainy Baby?

"The concept of childhood, so vital to the traditional American way of life, is threatened with extinction in the society we have created. Today's child has become the unwilling, unintended victim of overwhelming stress—the stress borne of rapid, bewildering social change and constantly rising expectations."

With those words, Dr. David Elkind began *The Hurried Child.* The book was written more than twenty years ago, but its words still ring true. The pressure to succeed on an adult level is starting at an earlier and earlier age. Parents have a hard time resisting the temptation to push their preschooler because much of what they read and hear about in books and the media only reinforces their insecurity about their own success as parents.

Some of this "expert" advice encourages parents to begin pushing children while they are still in the womb. In *How to Have a Smarter Baby: The Infant Stimulation Program for Enhancing Your Baby's Natural Development,* Susan Ludington-Hoe and Susan K. Golant advise people to make prenatal tapes of themselves talking to their unborn children and then to play them to the unborn child. They say this activity will help the fetus "bond" to its parents from the moment of birth.

Ludington-Hoe and Golant tell the story of one couple who made a tape of their voices and, when the mom was seven months pregnant, began playing it daily through stereo headphones placed on the mom's lower abdomen, "near [the baby's] ears." When the baby was born, the dad immediately began repeating the phrases he had spoken into the tape recorder. Lo and behold, at "the first sound of [the dad's] voice," the baby "lifted his head and turned to the left to find the source of the familiar intonations! As long as [the dad] talked, [the baby] maintained his gaze in his father's direction.

"Then, during a pause, [the dad] moved to the other side of the delivery table and repeated the sentences again. [The baby] lifted his little head once more and turned it 180 degrees to find [his dad] on the other side! In fact, whenever [the dad] changed positions, uttering the same phrases, the baby turned his head."

The authors also tell the story of an obstetrician

named Dr. F. Rene Van de Carr, who asked his pregnant patients to tape record themselves saying, "Ha, ha, ha, ha . . ." and play it back to their fetuses during the last two months of pregnancy.

"Nothing prepared him for what [actually happened]. After the delivery, Dr. Van de Carr had instructed his patients to call him if they noticed anything unusual. Well, several mothers reported that their four-day-old newborns were making very distinct sounds! In fact, the parents heard their babies say, 'Haha . . . Haha . . . Haha.'"

Just in case you were beginning to feel guilty for not reading Shakespeare aloud while you (or your wife) were waiting for your baby to make an appearance, Ludington-Hoe offers her own line of stimulation toys, as well as a stimulation program that sounds like it came straight out of a manual from baby boot camp. She offers smell games, touch games, positional exercises and all kinds of other rigidly timed activities that are supposed to stimulate your baby's brain cells.

Talk about programming and overscheduling at an early age! Ludington-Hoe and Golant don't say whether this program will ensure admission to Harvard, but the title of their book, *How to Have a Smarter Baby*, certainly implies that the odds will increase for children who follow their program.

Then there's *Super Baby: Boost Your Baby's Potential from Conception to Year One* in which Dr. Sarah Brewer "gives parents practical ways to boost their baby's intelligence. This includes playing musical rhythms to provide a stimulating womb environment, eating the right foods to help your baby's brain develop, taking gentle exercise to improve the flow of oxygenated blood to your baby's brain."

These authors are by no means alone in encouraging parents to push their preschoolers. Hurrying influences are everywhere. One newspaper article instructs parents on "How sign language may boost babies' IQ: signing may make infants happier today, smarter tomorrow."[1] Another article talks about "Math & music: the magical connection. Math and music unite the two hemispheres of the brain—a powerful force for learning."[2]

A Web site sells InfantStim T-shirts with black-and-white graphics and line-drawn faces on the front. The Web site contains research showing that infants prefer these graphics, but it doesn't stop there. The promotion claims that these graphics "not only attract a baby's attention, but can actually help increase their cognitive development."[3]

Videos like "Baby Shakespeare," "Your Baby Can Read!" and "Brainy Baby," which promises to "actually make your child smarter," and flash cards and CDs are available, too. Home learning programs (like "Hooked on Phonics") guarantee better grades in school while cassette courses promise to teach your preschooler Spanish, German or French.

Of course, computer programs (like "Jumpstart Baby") have spawned a new genre of software called "lapware" because it is intended for children so small that they have to sit on adults' laps to use the computer. That small inconvenience has not hindered sales. Lapware is now one of the fastest growing segments of the software industry. Sales of lapware programs have doubled since 1997.

If you think you're not doing enough by just wearing stimulating T-shirts or playing computer games, you can always send your child to an "Ivy League" preschool—they are popping up in a number of states across America. One of them, called Crème de la Crème, has schools in Colorado, Texas and Georgia. In Denver, Crème de la Crème has a waiting list of parents who are willing and eager to pay fourteen thousand dollars a year in tuition for the opportunity to enroll their children. Fourteen thousand dollars for preschool! Obviously, this place is no ordinary preschool. The lucky three-year-olds who are accepted may be just out of diapers, but they receive daily French lessons, cavort in the dance studio or the art gallery, and eat lunches of salmon patties, garlic mashed potatoes and legumes. Crème de la Crème is one of a growing number of preschool programs designed to produce little Einsteins.

Fancy preschools don't corner the market on programs that claim to enhance a young child's intellectual stimulation. Government has also entered the act. Two states, Georgia and Tennessee, send a classical music CD to the home of every newborn in an attempt to take advantage of the so-called "Mozart effect," whereby exposure to classical music supposedly enhances children's intellectual development.

In the Name of Science

These products and programs have arisen from an explosion of data coming out of neuroscience labs studying the way nerve cell connections, called synapses, form in young children's brains. Unfortunately, the public often misunderstands the data, which became evident to me when I heard a number of parents use almost the same words as they tried to explain their actions: "If we don't stimulate them in the first few years, they'll start to lose brain cell connections. And once those connections are gone, they're gone for good."

One Web site describes this "more is better" belief well: "The amount of stimulation your baby receives has a direct effect on how many synapses are formed. Repetitive stimulation strengthens these connections and makes them permanent, whereas young connections that don't get used eventually die out.

"These first years are a very important and pivotal time for a developing young brain. This intense period of brain growth and network-building happens only once in a lifetime. We as parents have a brief but golden opportunity to help our babies stimulate the formation of brain circuitry."[4]

Dr. John Bruer calls this "the myth of the first three years," the belief that parents can create a brilliant child if only they provide enough stimulation. The problem is that no good evidence supports this belief. The myth is mostly based on studies of animals exposed to periods of extreme environmental deprivation that have virtually no relevance to American families today. As one scientist has pointed out, "The difference between enriched and severely deprived is very different than the difference, as most parents extrapolate, between a good and a great environment."[5]

Media coverage doesn't help parents understand this difference. A *Time* magazine cover story in 1997 told parents, "Starting shortly after birth, a baby's brain, in a display of biological exuberance, produces trillions more connections between neurons than it can possibly use. Then, through a process that resembles Darwinian competition, the brain eliminates connections, or synapses, that are seldom or never used."

The article continued, "Not only do young rats reared in toy-strewn cages exhibit more complex behavior than rats confined to sterile, uninteresting boxes, researchers at the University of Illinois at Urbana-Champaign have found, but the brains of these rats contain as many as 25 percent more synapses per neuron. Rich experiences, in other words, really do produce rich brains."[6]

Human beings are very different than laboratory rats, and the leap from basic scientific research to real world application is a long one. But while a child's development can be harmed under conditions of extreme deprivation, virtually no evidence exists to support the converse: that you can enhance brain development through intensive stimulation.

Such stimulation can, in fact, be harmful. One two-year-old girl named Paula developed chronic diarrhea because of constant pressure from her parents. They would make Paula look at flash cards for at least an hour each day to try to "get her to speak better." Paula's pediatrician thought she spoke at an appropriate level for her age, but "appropriate" wasn't enough for Paula's parents. They wanted her to be "prepared for kindergarten," before she had even started preschool!

After many weeks of cajoling, the pediatrician finally persuaded Paula's parents to stop their flash card routine. They were surprised, and embarrassed, to see the diarrhea stop within a few days. They had never imagined that their efforts to "prepare" their daughter would make her physically ill.

Dr. Elkind calls parents like Paula's "college-degree" parents. He says, "Part of the 'superkid' psychology is that parents play an important part in getting their children to excel. By getting their young

child into an academically oriented preschool and/or
by teaching the child to read early, 'college-degree'
parents hope to give their child superior intellectual
ability."[7]

My wife and I almost bought into this madness.
When our son, Jacob, entered kindergarten, he was
one to two grade levels ahead in his math skills but,
as was normal for a kid his age, he had not yet
started to read. We figured we would try to give him
a jump-start, so we bought early reader books,
played rhyming games, and generally tried to stimulate his interest in letters and words. His teacher
told us he was interested in these things in class and
was doing well with them, but at home, nothing.

At first we became a little concerned. Every time
we took out the early reader books, Jacob told us
curtly, "I don't want to do that." After he rebuffed us
a few times, we realized that Jacob just wasn't
ready, and we decided to back off and wait until he
showed interest in reading on his own.

Four months later, Jacob came to us and said, "I
want to learn how to read." We weren't sure what
suddenly sparked his interest, but that night my wife
again took out the early reader books and taught our
son how to sound out words. Within two weeks, he
was reading the whole series of books by himself! All
we had to do was wait for him to be ready. If we had
pushed harder, earlier, we could easily have derailed
his natural developmental progression and damaged
his self-esteem.

Some college-degree parents take this accelera-
tion one step further. The Polks are one example.
Intellectual achievement was not their only incentive
to push their preschoolers. They enrolled their
five-year-old and three-year-old sons in Chinese

language classes so they "will be successful in business when they grow up." The children also have private tutors for their regular coursework to make sure they stay "at least a grade level ahead of where their friends are," according to Mr. Polk.

Having your child learn a foreign language is a laudable goal. In fact, research indicates that young children who are taught a foreign language are more likely to speak it without an accent than children who learn when they are older. However, is it really healthy to push a preschooler to learn a foreign language because we think it will help make him rich thirty years down the road? Is that the message we want to send to our children?

The Polk children are undeniably bright, and their parents are justifiably proud. They are well behaved and seemingly mature for their ages. They may be able to handle the academic pressure. Then again, maybe not. Often the results of such chronic stress aren't seen until children are well past the preschool stage.

Hundreds, if not thousands, of New York City kids may have to deal with these consequences as their parents grill them so they will be accepted to the "right" preschool. In a 1999 cover story entitled, "What Your Four-Year-Old Doesn't Know Could Ruin His Life," *New York* magazine showed the lengths to which parents will go to keep from "ruining" their children's lives. Many private kindergartens test a child's IQ as part of their admissions screening process. Some parents try to obtain an advantage by hiring a psychologist to run their child through the IQ test before they take it for real.

One family, the Marlowes, hired a psychologist after their four-year-old daughter, Jackie, scored only "moderately well" on the test the first time she took it. The child had three sessions a week with the psychologist. In addition, whenever Jackie had free time, her parents made her study for the test, all the time looking over her shoulder to make sure she was working hard.

In a short time, the pressure became too much for Jackie to bear. She couldn't sleep at night and kept complaining that she didn't feel well and didn't want to go to school. Still, her parents pressed her to study for her entrance exams.

On the day of the exam, the Marlowes were very hopeful that Jackie would score well enough to get into a good school. She didn't. Although her scores improved slightly, they still didn't meet the criteria of most schools. Her parents were devastated.

"We had such high hopes," Mrs. Marlowe told a friend. "We thought her entire future was wrapped up in that test. We were shortsighted." Jackie ended up attending one of the "non–Ivy League" private schools, and flourished.

"She's doing so well in school and is so happy," her mom said. "If I could go back in time, I would have laid off and not been so neurotic. I guess I didn't stop to think that maybe I was expecting her to be someone she wasn't. Don't get me wrong, she's very smart. She just wanted to be a kid, but I was pressuring her like she was an adult."

When Push Comes to Shove

Some parents can't tell the difference between gently pushing a child to reach the peak of his potential and shoving him so hard that he falls into an abyss of unfulfilled expectations. When a child falls into that abyss at a very young age, climbing back out becomes difficult. Evidence shows that trying to force too much into a child's mind too soon can result in delays of essential skills such as reading. He can also end up liking school less, being less creative, having behavioral problems and perhaps suffering from the psychosomatic complaints typical of burnout.[8]

The potentially harmful effects of too much parental pressure don't end in the preschool classroom. A push often becomes a shove on the ball field, too. Alan L. knows this effect all too well. He told me his mother was the "epitome of a tennis mother." She first put a racket in his hand when he was only four or five years old. Then she forced him to play. And play. And play.

"She was always pushing me very hard," Alan said. "I remember playing at night when it was starting to get dark out but she would constantly say, 'Three more, three more.' And we'd hit the three balls and again she'd yell, 'Three more.' And I would tell her, 'It's enough. It's getting dark out.' It didn't matter. All I kept hearing was, 'Three more, three more.' Every night she made me stay out there for an extra twenty minutes."

In one respect, Alan's mother's prodding paid off. By ten years old, he was one of the top-ranked young players in New England. Yet such an achievement wasn't good enough for his mother.

"If I was playing in a tournament and I was seeded third and my opponent was seeded eighth, I was expected to win. God forbid I lost a match to someone seeded below me, I'd catch hell. Literally, on the ride home, I would hear point by point by point what I did wrong, every single point, over and over again. I was a ten-year-old kid and would be in tears but would continue to hear point by point what I did wrong. At some point, when I was eleven or twelve, I would throw up before every tournament. It would invariably happen the night before the tournament started. I couldn't control it."

Alan continued to play—he had no choice, really—but a long time went by before he was able to enjoy his athletic success.

"My mother passed away when I was fourteen. I ultimately gave up tennis at that point for a year or two. I needed to get away from it. When I was eighteen and in high school I started playing competitively again and finally started to enjoy it. For the first time in my life, I was doing it for myself as opposed to anyone else."

Alan now has children of his own. He told me that he would love it if at least one of his kids wanted to play tennis. He is encouraging them, but he won't force them. Alan has learned the lesson that his mother failed to heed: You can often achieve more with a gentle push than you can with a hard shove.

A soft touch can also keep a young kid from getting hurt physically. Cartilage in growing children is softer than in adults and has a greater chance of injury. The same goes for bones. In contact sports, injuries to the growth plates—the portion of the bones responsible for growth—are common.

"This risk may be increasing because these young players are now training harder and playing more intensely," says Dr. Lyle Micheli, a physician in the Division of Sports Medicine at Children's Hospital in Boston.[9]

In many cases, growth plate fractures in young children can cause the bone to grow slowly or to stop growing prematurely. The result could be a limb that is shorter than the opposite, uninjured limb. If only part of the growth plate is injured, growth may be lopsided and the limb may be crooked.

Broken bones are only one problem with pushing preschool athletes too hard. Surprisingly, noncontact sports can be almost as dangerous for young children. Up to half of all pediatric sports injuries result from overuse. When a young, growing child repeatedly exercises specific parts of his body—for example, throwing a baseball, serving a tennis ball or kicking a soccer ball—the muscles, tendons and bones become fatigued. If they are not given time to rest and recover, they develop microtrauma. Recurrent microtrauma can add up to debilitating injuries, weakness, loss of flexibility and chronic pain—before a child even reaches puberty.

UCLA orthopedist John DiFiori says, "Pressure from others, especially adults, may play a role in the development of overuse injury. Parents and coaches who promote excessive intensity or who encourage a 'no pain, no gain' or win-at-all-costs attitude may contribute to injury."[10]

Sooner or Later

We've been conditioned to think that sooner is usually better. How many times have you heard a parent brag that their toddler can already speak, or that their three-year-old can swim like a fish? Worse yet, how many times have you felt insecure about your own preschooler's abilities because another child seemed to be progressing faster? I know I have. In our competitive culture, such a reaction is natural, but it's wrong.

The Harvard Preschool Project is the most exten-
sive study on early learning ever performed. Dr.
Michael Meyerhoff was part of the Harvard research
team that looked at what successful students did
early in their schooling. In a story that first appeared
on *NBC Nightly News,* Dr. Meyerhoff said, "As it
turned out, they weren't doing flash cards; they
weren't doing drills; they weren't exposed to anything specifically academic in nature."[11] Meyerhoff
said that what the successful children did was play.
Just playing—no fancy games, toys, classes and gadgets—helped kids' brains develop and laid the foundation for their future success. "Your Thomas
Edison, your Bill Gates—those kind of people who
have really made substantial breakthroughs—when
they are asked, 'How did you come up with the
idea?' invariably they'll respond, 'Oh, I was playing
around with this.' They know how to play,"
Meyerhoff added.

Dr. Elkind echoes this notion that the playground
may be the best classroom for young children:
"Parents have this misconception somehow that
education is a race and the earlier you start, the better you finish. The whole problem is they think
they're giving their kids a head start by starting
them early and that somehow that head start is
going to be a lasting advantage. But that's simply the
wrong analogy. Education is not a race. There's no
starting point and end point."[12]

They're going to make it, sooner or later. Children
develop at different speeds. They also develop different aptitudes. Some will be good at math; others
will have trouble adding and subtracting but will be
good with a paintbrush. We can't force these out-
comes on our children, no matter how hard we try.

However, you can set your children on a path that will help them reach their own individual potential.

Match Your Child's Tasks to Her Developmental Stage

One story makes me shake my head whenever I think about it.

A mother called her pediatrician to ask for a referral to a learning specialist to help her four-year-old daughter learn the alphabet. The reason? The preschool she had chosen for her daughter required it. According to the pediatrician, the child was "normal in every way. She had a normal intelligence and was developing normally. But she just wasn't ready to read yet."

The pediatrician explained this to the mother and recommended that she enroll her child in another school, one that would let her develop at her own pace. However, that suggestion didn't satisfy the woman. The school's requirements made her feel that her child was falling behind other children, so she spent her entire summer vacation trying to teach her daughter the alphabet. It didn't work. "No matter how hard the mom tried to shove letters down her throat," said the pediatrician, "the kid's brain wasn't mature enough to take them all in. I feel bad for her. I can just imagine the inferiority complex she's going to have when she grows up."

That's only one example of a parent pushing a child to do something his body or mind won't yet let him do. Others are less obvious. I know many parents who sit their two-year-old children in front of the television to watch *Sesame Street* in the hope they will begin to learn the alphabet. While Big Bird and Elmo may entertain these toddlers, these characters will not likely teach such young children the alphabet. Nor will a parent make a child smarter by forcing the alphabet upon him.

Even the creators of *Sesame Street* agree: "When parents hear about the importance of stimulation, they may wonder whether they should be making special efforts to encourage their baby's intellectual growth. In other words, will more stimulation result in an even smarter baby?

"Most experts believe that it doesn't help to pressure babies and young children to learn. In fact, pressure can turn learning into a source of anxiety. Patricia Goldman-Rakic, Ph.D., professor of neuroscience at Yale University School of Medicine, adds, 'Young minds can absorb information efficiently, but the child must be ready for it.' Parents must be careful not to frustrate a child by pushing him to perform tasks that are beyond his level. 'And don't be concerned about how well a young child performs a task,' Dr. Goldman-Rakic adds. 'There's no question that he will master it over time.'"[13]

"The key to the preschool and toddler years," says Dr. Jim Loomis, "is to find out where your children are and provide them developmentally appropriate challenges. For some kids, pushing them to read early is fine because they love to read. But for the kid who can't, it does two things: it sends the parent going around saying, 'My kid's a failure, my kid's a failure,' which eventually undermines the bond with the kid and can undermine the kid's self-esteem; and it also makes it very frustrating when everyone is putting a book in front of him saying, 'See this letter, see this letter.' If they're not developmentally ready for it, it just kills motivation."[14]

Preschool children develop at different rates. Some children will be way ahead in certain tasks because they have developed those skills faster, which doesn't necessarily mean they are smarter. Other kids may very well "catch up" the next year when their development allows. Just as with the tortoise and the hare, the late bloomer may eventually surpass the early bird.

One man I spoke to described another peril of pushing a preschooler: "My son read at four years old. He could do basic arithmetic, too. I tried too hard and pushed a little and gave him a lot of information that he didn't need at that time.

"Now at eleven years old, he's always bored. He doesn't enjoy life as all his friends do. He says that school is boring and that everything he learns there, he already knew.

"I think now that there's a time for everything, and each thing has its own correct time. There is a time to be child and a time to play and to discover life."

You Are the Best Teacher

Videos, flash cards, classes, tapes, *Sesame Street*. None of these things will make your child smarter or develop faster, and none of them are as good for your preschooler's healthy development as the hours spent with Mom or Dad. Indeed, if these activities take away from the time you spend with your child, they could impede his development.

All the available scientific research says that we should do what comes naturally when we are with our babies: talk, play and make funny faces. Young children are programmed to respond to our doting attention.

Zero to Three is a national organization formed to try to strengthen and support families and to promote the healthy development of babies and toddlers. This group's Web site states, "The task for parents and other caregivers who want their children to succeed in school is not to force development. Rather, it is to try to ensure that the moment-to-moment events of daily life give babies and toddlers the sense of security, encouragement and confidence that are the foundation of emotional health. It is this that will ultimately allow them to learn at home, in school and throughout life."[15]

Preschool Is Optional

A big push is on in our society to enroll children in school as early as possible. We are told that preschool will help our children develop, both socially and intellectually. This correlation may hold for underprivileged children, who score better on math tests if they've attended preschool. "But there's no evidence that [preschool] makes a significant difference in the ultimate academic success of middle-class kids," says David Grissmer, author of the RAND study "Why Pupils Excel."[16]

Dr. Elkind says, "When we instruct children in academic subjects, or in swimming, gymnastics, or ballet, at too early an age, we miseducate them; we put them at risk for short-term stress and long-term personality damage for no useful purpose. There is no evidence that such early instruction has lasting benefits and considerable evidence that it can do lasting harm."[17]

Working parents may have no choice but to send their children to preschool. My wife and I both work, and all of our three children have attended or will attend preschool. However, we were careful to choose a preschool that did not teach academic subjects to the children. Instead, the preschool lets children participate in activities that are geared toward each child's developmental level.

Families with a stay-at-home parent may have more options. Preschool is one possibility; keeping the child home with Mom or Dad is another. Your child will learn as much, or more, spending time with you as she would in a classroom. Everyday activities provide the stimulation necessary to work those brain cells, so don't feel pressured to send your child to preschool. Do it because you want to, not because you think you have to.

As one psychologist has said, "It isn't imperative to have them in an organized setting for learning. If you let them help you take dishes out of the dishwasher when they're three, they're learning."[18]

Don't Get Sucked In by Advertising or "Science"

When our third child, A. J., was born, we received our share of baby gifts. We were given lots of clothing and other necessities. But our friends and family also gave us black-and-white cards to tape on the wall above the changing table to stimulate the baby; books containing different textured objects for the baby to feel; a colorful mobile to hang above the crib; a CD called "Baby Mozart: Music to Stimulate

Your Baby's Brain"; a crib bumper with a built-in musical keyboard so that when the baby kicked a key, the bumper would play a musical note; and toys with patterned drawings, sounds, whirligigs and other components designed to stimulate A. J.'s brain.

Our family and friends were certainly generous and well-meaning. Most of them gave these gifts in the belief that they could help stimulate our child and thus make him smarter than he would otherwise be. However, they are victims of the media and commercial hype surrounding research into brain development.

John Bruer, in his book, *The Myth of the First Three Years: A New Understanding of Early Brain Development and Lifelong Learning*, does a masterful job of detailing the way the media and the public misunderstand and misuse neuroscience data. He says, "Brain science has not pointed to new ways of raising or teaching children that will really stimulate those synapses above and beyond what normal experiences provide."

That message hasn't reached the public. I performed an informal, unscientific poll among my friends to find out how many of them had heard about the so-called "Mozart effect." Each person I asked had heard of it, and most of them believed that playing Mozart for a baby would help make the child smarter. And why not? *Scholastic Parent & Child* magazine assures us that, "In recent years, there has been a considerable amount of research on the effect of music on brain development and thinking. Neurological research has found that the higher brain functions of abstract reasoning as well as spatial and temporal conceptualization are enhanced by music activities. Activities with music can generate the neural connections necessary for using important math skills."[19]

Of course, other sources rave about the magic of Mozart. Parenting magazines, newspapers, advertisements, state legislatures and governors have jumped on the Mozart bandwagon. However, Dr. Bruer points out that the people who originally touted the Mozart effect, ". . . confused the results of a study on how listening to classical music affects college students' reasoning skills (for periods up to ten minutes) with the results of a study on the effects of musical keyboard lessons given to preschoolers (where spatial reasoning skills appeared to improve for several hours after the lesson)." The bottom line: no evidence supports the claim that listening to classical CDs improves childrens' spatial reasoning skills.

The facts haven't stopped corporate America from trying to cash in on the misperception. Companies spend millions of dollars propagating the myth that more stimulation means more baby brainpower. Companies making educational videos, CDs, computer software and toys want us to believe this myth, which infuriates some child development experts, including Matthew Melamud, executive director of Zero to Three: "To translate that research into specific products to boost babies' brainpower is really an abomination, a commercial abomination."[20]

"You can buy the black-and-white, Calder-like mobile to hang over the crib if you want," says Dr. Bruer. "It may amuse you and may even amuse the baby. But it won't make the infant see either better or earlier than it would otherwise. You can play Mozart softly in the nursery, but it won't make your baby hear better or earlier than it would normally."

So don't get sucked in by all the hype and advertising. Science has not shown us how to create a super-child. In fact, science has shown instead that the things parents have been doing since the beginning of time are the very things that help a child develop into a healthy, intelligent and happy adult.

Loving your child, spending time with him, showing that you care, and taking an active role in his life is the best way to promote brainpower, and it doesn't cost anything.

Know Your Child's "Physical Fitness"

It seems obvious that a five-year-old, aspiring Little Leaguer shouldn't be throwing curve balls. But should he be throwing at all? Overuse injuries are rampant among preschoolers, and our job is to prevent them.

I recently heard about one parent with a five-year-old son who is very interested in sports, especially soccer. The boy played almost every day after school with the kids in the neighborhood. After a few months, though, he began to complain of chronic pain in his right knee, his dominant kicking leg.

The child was told to take a break from soccer, and it worked. The pain slowly disappeared. The orthopedist told the parents that the repetitive kicking motion put too much stress on the child's growing tendons and cartilage. His young frame just needed a chance to rest and recover.

The child is back to playing soccer, but his parents limit him to a few days a week. He is allowed to play other sports on his soccer-free days. The variety provides a built-in rest period, even while the child plays another sport.

If you set limits and encourage variety, you can prevent overuse injuries in your child. Before that, however, you should make sure that your child is physically fit to play the sport she chooses. The best way to find out is to consult a pediatrician before your child begins to participate in a sport.

Also, make sure your child is interested in the sport you want her to play. Forcing a child into a sport she doesn't like sets her up for failure and disappointment, perhaps damaging a child's self-esteem and turning her away from sports forever. Remember that you're signing your child up for the sport, not you! Pushing a preschooler into a sport too early is the quickest way to stifle any chance that he may be interested in that sport in the future.

Not All Educational Programs Are Bad

So, you want to help your child read better? Nothing is inherently wrong with the Phonics Game, flash cards or "Reader Rabbit "computer programs. These tools are only harmful if they are used inappropriately, which means that you have to understand your child's intellectual and emotional stage of development. In general, I believe that if you have high expectations, a child will rise to meet them. Trouble occurs when a parent sets the bar so high that the child cannot reach it. The right educational aid can help a child reach his potential; the wrong one can damage self-esteem.

If you do want to use some of the commercially available educational products, you can take a number of practical steps to help ensure that you use them appropriately. "Education should be a partnership between the parent and the teacher," says Lynne Drabkin, former director of gifted programs in a New York City community school district. "Parents should consult with their child's teacher before choosing and implementing an educational support program."[21]

Drabkin says one way to determine if an educational program is appropriate is to ask yourself whether or not it is fun: "The whole experience should be a pleasant one for the parent and the child. Children should, generally speaking, not be resistant to the process. If a child becomes frustrated, it may be that the material is too difficult, he is not emotionally ready to be pressed ahead or the particular approach of the program may be wrong." Most children will instinctively recoil against a learning process that is too onerous.

If you want to use an educational program, don't pay attention to the advertising. Just because the ad says the tool is appropriate for a five-year-old child doesn't mean that it's appropriate for *your* five-year-old. So take your time, observe your child, analyze his capabilities, compare them to your expectations and then choose a program that he will find both enriching and enjoyable.

EIGHT

IT'S ACADEMIC

Yin-Yang

For many years, American parents and politicians have envied the Japanese educational system, where schools have a reputation for requiring long hours of a curriculum that places a heavy emphasis on the basics, such as math and science. The result: Japanese students score better than American students on most standardized tests; they are more disciplined; there are fewer behavioral problems.

However, all is not well in Japanese schools; Japanese children have paid a price for their academic success. In a 1998 report, the United Nations Committee on the Rights of the Child urged the Japanese government to establish an independent monitoring mechanism to protect children's rights. The committee said, "In view of the highly competitive educational system existing in the state and its consequent negative effects on children's physical and mental health, the committee recommends the state . . . take appropriate steps to prevent and combat excessive stress and school phobia."[1]

Japan's answer has been a radical (for them) restructuring of the country's educational system in order to take some pressure off their children. "We are going to try the sunshine approach, giving them more chances to play sports or read books," Ken Terawaki, a senior Education Ministry official, told the *New York Times*. "We would like to give them some free time and the psychological freedom to do things that they are interested in. In other words, we want to give them some time to think, rather than force everybody to stay in school to study the same thing."[2]

Many Japanese parents and educators oppose the restructuring plan. Although the curriculum changes are scheduled to begin in 2002, Japanese officials are running into a problem that sounds all too American: parents worry that the changes will make their children less competitive.

Ryoko Zaitsu sends her seventh-grade son to a private school and hires an academic tutor for him, rather than take the chance that this sunshine approach will make him fall behind his classmates.

"'It shouldn't be necessary, but other parents will keep sending their children, so you feel that you have to, too,' says Ms. Zaitsu. 'Frankly speaking, I would like to start a revolt. But not everyone feels that way, so we are left with a feeling of helplessness. You want to do something but you can't move. In the end, you feel that you just have to take care of yourself.'"[3]

The Paradox

While the Japanese are striving to deemphasize academic pressure and foster creativity in their children, we in America seem to be doing the converse. We are turning our schools into cyclones of stress, which may be stifling our kids' creativity. We are the yin to their yang.

One survey found that 91 percent of American parents believe play is important to the overall well-being of their children.[4] Almost half of parents said play contributed to their own success as adults; they also felt strongly that the educational system places too much emphasis on grades and has become too competitive.

So far, so good. But the survey went on to reveal that 72 percent of parents think that children starting their academic learning early is very important, and 54 percent believe that the academic setting already includes enough play time. Dr. Michael Cohen, president of the company that conducted the survey, put it succinctly: "This survey clearly demonstrates that play and academics are on a collision course, and play is losing. While parents believe in the importance of play, they make decisions that sacrifice play in the hopes of academic success for their children."

Why can many of us talk the talk, but we can't walk the walk? We understand the destructive effects of stress, yet we place increasing amounts of academic pressure on our children. We acknowledge the importance of play, yet we readily sacrifice play for more academics. We know that perfection is impossible, yet many of us are unwilling to accept that our children can't always bring home a perfect report card. We celebrate diversity, yet we refuse to recognize that not every child will be a straight-A student, no matter how hard he tries. Indeed, we seem to be pushing our children harder, longer and at an earlier age, despite the fact that we know it's not necessarily in their best interest.

One reason for this paradox is that in America,

education is the road to success. As competition increases to gain acceptance into the best schools, to land the best jobs and to make the most money, parents are increasingly willing to let their child's health and happiness take a back seat to the quest for academic superiority.

Harvard's dean of admissions and financial aid has seen firsthand the destructive effects of this academic pressure. He writes, "The chase for the prize begins early on. . . . Sports, music, dance and other recreational activities used to provide a welcome break, a time to relax and unwind. No more: training for college scholarships, or professional contracts, begins early, even in grammar school. . . . Summer vacations have become a thing of the past. The pace of the day and the year allows little time simply 'to be a kid,' or, it seems, to develop into a complete human being."[5]

Schools contribute to this cycle of stress. Kim, a kindergarten teacher for eleven years, worries that two specific educational trends will have the unintended consequence of increasing pressure on students: the trend toward year-round schools and the elimination of recess. "Year-round school has not reached our small Southern town yet, but it is in a neighboring town," she writes. "We have, however, had our recess reduced to twenty minutes. That's hardly enough time to get them outside and then round them up and get them organized to go back inside.

"The curriculum is so intense that teachers have a hard time scheduling free time in the classroom. Some of the children have had their lives so scheduled that they don't know what to do when they do have free time. I've seen this at 'free center time' when children wander aimlessly around the room unable to choose an activity."[6]

Decreasing school "free time" may also decrease a child's academic performance. Research out of the University of Georgia has shown that children concentrate better in class if they've had time during recess to "let off steam" that builds up when they sit at their desks for a long time.

Hannah Sun knows firsthand how important being able to relax is when there's so much pressure for academic success. Unfortunately, her parents don't feel the same way. Hannah is a student at Lynbrook High School in California. She says, "Summer is supposed to be fun and relaxing. But every morning at eight, my mom comes into my room and yells at me to get up and do my homework and study for the SATs. Now, it helps having someone to remind you what you still need to get done. But not at 8 A.M. when you can be sleeping until ten or eleven! There is always endless nagging and studying to do."

Hannah's parents are Chinese. She says most of her Chinese-American friends complain that their parents pressure them to come home with perfect report cards. She blames it on the "strict education and discipline" they were subjected to growing up in their home country. But millions of American children of all backgrounds and nationalities share Hannah's experience.

"I hate disappointing my parents when I bring home a report card with Bs on it," Hannah says. "I hate how they threaten to make me quit my extracurricular activities if I don't study more. . . . Right now, even though I'm involved in a million extracurricular activities, I enjoy everything I'm doing. I probably won't have a chance to do these things when I enter college, so this is one chance in a lifetime that I have to hold on to.

"My life won't be ruined if I don't get into Berkeley. . . . Most Asian parents have to realize that life isn't just about studying, going to a famous college and being rich. I know they want their children to have the very best, but sometimes the pressure backfires. I know of some Chinese-American students in high school who have committed suicide because they just couldn't handle the pressure anymore."[7]

Between 1980 and 1992, the suicide rate for children fifteen to nineteen years of age increased by 28.3 percent. Academic stress is not the only factor to blame for this epidemic of teen suicide, but pressure undoubtedly plays a role. In fact, one survey by Childline UK Charity indicates that "the pressure on children to succeed academically is so great that some children as young as seven consider suicide."[8]

Adherents of Chinese Taoism believe that yin and yang are two opposite energies that, by their fluctuation and interaction, are the cause of the universe and all phenomena that take place within it. In this belief system, yin-yang is seen as a cyclic process; when something reaches an extreme stage, it transforms into its opposite.[9] Although I am not a follower of Taoism, I can think of no better example of this philosophy than when the pressure to achieve extraordinary success drives a child to commit suicide, life's ultimate failure.

The Price of "Success"

Suicide is the most dramatic, if least common, sign of the academic stress many of us place on our children. One researcher says, "The best efforts of affluent, fast-track parents to produce academically successful children can spawn unintended negative consequences, such as stress disorders and cheating among children unable to cope with such pressure. Super-competitors have trouble forming close friendships, and their overscheduled parents lack sufficient time for nurturing."[10]

Aileen Dickey, an assistant principal at Antelope Trails Elementary School in Colorado Springs, Colorado, says she sees lots of kids who become ill and are continually in the office complaining of stomachaches and headaches. "These are kids who have stomach problems all the time, even to the point of vomiting. Sometimes they make themselves sick because their parents have put so much pressure on them."

Think of children like Jeremy, a fourth-grader who his teacher said was ". . . a nervous wreck. The pressure on him to perform in school was so great that in second grade he developed bleeding ulcers."

Take Kristen, a bright sixteen-year-old girl with epilepsy whose seizures were well controlled with medication for many years. When she entered high school, however, she started having seizures again. As her condition worsened, Kristen's doctors eventually noticed a pattern. The seizures usually occurred when she had to take tests. Why? Her psychologist says Kristen was a good student, but her test scores were never high enough to satisfy her parents, both of whom were demanding, Ivy League-educated physicians. They had been straight-A students, and they expected the same from their daughter.

With a lot of psychological counseling, Kristen has finally learned to deal with the stress, despite the fact that her parents have been unable to change their behavior. Kristen's seizures occur much less frequently now, and she continues to perform well in school.

Like most kids, Kristen knew the importance of good grades without her parents telling her. According to one poll, 76 percent of all teenagers say their biggest stress comes from the classroom.[11] In a survey conducted by Shell Oil for the U.S. Department of Education, 44 percent of teenagers said "the pressure to get good grades," was one of their greatest concerns, while 32 percent cited "the pressure to get into college."[12] Teenagers ranked these academic concerns higher than concerns about the pressure to fit in socially (29 percent), to use drugs or alcohol (19 percent), or to be sexually active (13 percent).

These studies reinforce what those of us who have children already know. Parenting isn't easy. It's more art than science, and part of that art involves knowing when to push your child and when to hold back. Connecticut Children's Medical Center's Dr. Jim Loomis says, "Some kids need a high bar and need a verbal kick in the behind at the same time. Some kids really need that structure. You give them that high bar and they do very well. Other kids just don't do well with that. You leave them alone and they do just fine. In fact, the more you interfere and the more you push, the more they struggle with it."

Steve was one of those children who did well on his own. He was a sophomore attending one of the finest private high schools in New Mexico. He was popular, active in student government and a straight-A student. One day, however, his parents came to speak to him about his schoolwork. They told him they were concerned because he "wasn't doing it right." Despite his grades, they felt Steve "wasn't studying as much" as he should have been.

Steve was shocked and upset by his parents' complaints. He had thought that his parents would take pride in his academic performance. Instead, they just found another reason to criticize him. When Steve realized his parents would never be satisfied, he began to withdraw. According to his psychologist, "There were a lot of conflicts and arguments. He didn't want to do anything his parents wanted him to do." Steve continued to rebel against his parents. Eventually, his grades began to suffer. Parental pressure had achieved the opposite of its intended effect, turning an enthusiastic A student into a mediocre one who lacked motivation.

"I've had lots and lots of kids completely sabotage their report cards, especially middle school and high school kids, because they're mad at their parents," says Dr. Sal Severe. Education expert June Million agrees that too much academic pressure can destroy a child's self-esteem, motivation and physical health. "Test pressure," she writes, "has resulted in high school students boycotting or intentionally failing tests and younger students becoming physically ill as test day approaches."[13]

Grades are important. They can tell us how our children are performing, how much they are learning or if they need extra help in certain subjects. However, too many of us have come to think that GPA. is short for "great person average," instead of "grade point average." We often mistake our child's school performance for a measure of what kind of a kid she is. If a child is a B student and achieves Bs on her report card, we may subconsciously think of her as less "successful" than her classmates who bring home As. Many parents will go to great lengths to change that perception.

A "Magic Bullet"

We live in an immediate gratification society. When we or someone we love is ill, our first instinct is to look for a miracle cure or to expect that doctors can eliminate the problem by prescribing a pill that works like a proverbial "magic bullet." This urge also extends to problems that aren't medical in origin. Our society has a tendency to "medicalize" many problems that are social or behavioral. If a problem is medical, people expect that some treatment is available. However, we've taken this viewpoint to an extreme. Seemingly everyone has depression, fibromyalgia, chronic Lyme disease, chronic fatigue syndrome, disc problems, chronic headaches, social anxiety disorder or some other chronic problem that keeps them from working, studying, striving or achieving what they want to achieve.

For children, the disease du jour is attention deficit/hyperactivity disorder—ADHD (or attention deficit disorder, ADD). Kids who genuinely suffer from this condition have trouble concentrating, sitting still, paying attention and completing tasks. However, many experts believe that thousands of children are being unnecessarily diagnosed with ADHD. They say these kids suffer nothing more than average school performance or the restlessness of childhood. Parents or teachers may view this "condition" as a problem, but it certainly doesn't require a medical diagnosis.

Still, giving a medical name to a behavioral or

social problem makes parents feel better, because if the problem is medical, parents can feel they have not failed in their job. If their child is "sick," then the parents can't be blamed for not producing a superchild.

"Every morning, a whistle sounds, letting kids at Kalamazoo Academy know it's time to leave the playground to go to class. Most students head straight for their classrooms, but roughly a dozen line up along the wall outside the principal's office," reports the *Detroit News*. "It's Ritalin time. Each student knows the routine, they do it every day. A student approaches the office counter, fills a plastic cup with his name on it with water. The office secretary searches a drawer for the prescription bottle or plastic bag with his name on it and drops a pill into his hand. He gulps down the pill, then returns the cup for tomorrow's dose."[14]

In another area of the country, the parents of a sixteen-year-old girl sit in their pediatrician's office insisting that their daughter has ADHD. The problem: the girl's school performance is only average in a town filled with above average children. The answer is the same as in Kalamazoo: Ritalin.

What is this wonder drug called Ritalin? It's an amphetamine-like stimulant similar to cocaine. Medical studies show that people who take Ritalin (or similar drugs that have names like Adderall and Concerta) concentrate better and can focus their minds more easily on a specific task. Many parents say their child's school performance improved dramatically after they started taking the medication. However, according to the federal Drug Enforcement Administration, more than one in every thirty American kids between the ages of five and nineteen now has a prescription for Ritalin. We Americans use five times as much Ritalin as the rest of the world!

Do we really want that many children hooked on stimulants? Do that many American children have brains that don't work properly? Could doctors have missed making the diagnosis of ADHD in millions of average children in previous generations? I doubt it. So does Helen Blackburn, an educational psychologist. She says, "Parents want a school-based reason why a child isn't doing well. And to say that a child is not bright, that they maybe are, it's an old-fashioned term, a 'slow learner,' or that there are family issues that are causing the problems in school, parents don't seem to want, they don't want to accept that. They want a diagnosis and a label that then makes the school responsible for solving the problem."[15]

Parents aren't the only ones to blame for this ADHD epidemic. Many doctors and psychologists are eager to make the diagnosis, and the schools themselves jump onto the bandwagon. Many experts claim that teachers and school administrators recommend children take Ritalin so they will be more docile and, hence, easier to control.

Matt Scherbel is one of these students. As an eighth-grader at Thomas Pyle Middle School in Bethesda, Maryland, he wrote in his school newspaper: "Schools don't like extremists who like to think and question. They are the dreamers. That doesn't mean that they are wrong. They just don't fit the norm, so they are labeled and damned, labeled as ADD (attention deficit disorder).

"Ritalin does not help me learn; it simply lowers my mind down between the selected lines in which we are taught. Who's going to get further in life, the schmo with the same textbook answers and ideas, or the 'ADD kid' who can offer ideas that have never been thought of or a new perspective on something?

"I truly look forward to the day when Ritalin isn't an answer. To the day when every student is labeled 'learner.'"[16]

Some concerned parents are fighting back against the ADHD establishment. In my own state of Connecticut, the legislature recently passed a bill banning any teacher, school counselor or school administrator from recommending that a child start taking Ritalin. The parents behind this reform bill hope it will decrease the number and occurrence of unnecessary prescriptions. I have spoken to many pediatricians, psychologists and psychiatrists who are also appalled by this ADHD epidemic. Many of them don't want to say it publicly for fear of angering some parents, but they agree with these efforts to keep normal kids from being treated as if they have some kind of disease.

Dr. Thomas Armstrong agrees this book, *The Myth of the ADD Child,* demonstrates that. "Not long ago, children who behaved in certain ways were called 'bundles of energy,' 'daydreamers,' or 'fireballs.' Now they're considered 'hyperactive,' 'distractible,' or 'impulsive,' victims of the ubiquitous attention deficit disorder. Tragically, such labeling can follow a child through life."[17]

Chasing "Success"

The answer may lie less in popping pills and more in redefining "success." Dr. John Friel says, "Many parents have a real narrow definition of intelligence and success. Unfortunately, a lot of the studies show that getting straight As is a good predictor of very little, especially success."[18] One such study, conducted at Harvard in the 1940s, showed that men who graduated with an A average were not particularly happy or successful ten years later. However, Harvard men who received mostly Bs were more successful and happier with their lives.

The disparity between grades and "success" is not limited to college students. Dr. Friel cites a study of all high school valedictorians in Indiana. Researchers tracked them down ten years after graduation and found that their academic success in high school predicted nothing. "Most of the high school valedictorians were not notable for anything," says Dr. Friel.

I know a lot of accomplished, happy people who were not star students, and I know plenty of Ivy League-educated, wealthy people who are unhappy. Who is more successful? The answer will probably determine whether we turn school into a cyclone of stress and our children into premature burnouts.

Can we help bring out the best in our children without making them sick? Can we push them to do well in school without burning them out? Can we maintain high aspirations for them without setting them up for failure and disappointment? The answer to all three of these questions is an emphatic, "Yes!" Here's how.

Have Realistic Expectations

The Uprights (not their real name) are a typical power couple. Mr. Upright is a state official; Mrs. Upright sits on a corporate board. Like many successful couples, they expected their son, William, to be successful, too.

The Uprights sent William to a competitive private school, which many other power children attended. William was a talented and creative kid who seemed to enjoy his new school. He studied hard and achieved a solid, if unspectacular, B average on his report cards. William was satisfied with his grades because he knew he had tried his hardest. His parents, however, didn't care how hard he had worked. They wanted to see As on his report card, and they made it clear to him that nothing less would do.

Not surprisingly, William's motivation to work hard in school suffered. He told his school counselor, "I am not going to play that game. Why should I work my tail off to get, at best, a B-plus, when I know that's not going to be good enough for my parents?" So instead, he goofed off in school. The more he goofed off, the more attention his parents gave him.

The Uprights viewed their son as a "failure" because he didn't live up to their unrealistic expectations. Dr. David Elkind says this problem is common. "I know too many kids who are B students and their parents want them to be A students and push them very hard. Well, they're already working as hard as they can. They're B students and they're always going to be B students, and that's okay. They're working at the top of their abilities and there's no reason to expect them to be something that they're not. You're not going to make a B student into an A student. I'm sorry. There are limits."

Assistant principal Aileen Dickey laughs when she says, "We joke that all new parents who come to the school bring a gifted child with them." But then she turns more serious. "It's the child who suffers because he feels like he's not living up to his parents' expectations. . . . The pressure that they get from their parents is devastating. They'll say, 'If you'd just work harder, it'll be good enough,' but I don't know if there's ever a 'good enough.' If the pressure gets high enough, the kid just turns off. He realizes he's never going to meet his parents' expectations, so he gives up. Otherwise, it's just continual failure. It breaks my heart."[19]

The Child's Heart Is Broken, Too

Dr. Elkind says most parents who raise happy, well-adjusted children "have been able to put their own egos aside and to observe those children and see what their interests are, what their abilities are and support those." He says that many parents often unwittingly put their own needs ahead of their kids'.[20]

Ironically, children often have the perspective that parents lack. Effie Varypatakis, a student at Chicopee High School in Chicopee, Massachusetts, says, "Many teens try their best, but sometimes that isn't good enough, and their parents will keep pressuring them to do better. Parents care a little too much about their kids having good grades. Every teen is different, and some have more ability than others, and therefore they get better grades."[21]

Nothing is wrong with wanting to challenge our children academically. The real issue is helpful challenge versus harmful challenge. Helpful challenges are based on a child's ability. That level might be above what they presently know and do but still is within the limits of their attainment. Harmful challenges expect the unachievable. Helpful challenges push kids to do their very best; harmful challenges push children down the road to stress and burnout.

We parents are leaders. If we want to guide our children toward academic achievement, we must do what all good leaders do: know the people we are leading. We have to know our children's strengths and weaknesses and build on them.

Emphasize Healthy Competition

Part of the problem with the way we measure academic success—grades and test scores—is that we are often measuring a child's performance against that of his classmates, which is probably the most divisive, least constructive way to measure a child's performance. Some extremely intelligent children can achieve As without trying very hard; other children will try as hard as they can and still bring home Bs. Should the smart but lazy child be praised at the expense of the hard-working, diligent B student?

That is what usually happens. In our competitive world, we tend to place the emphasis on winning rather than on playing as hard as you can. In reality, however, research shows that the most competitive kids are not necessarily the most successful ones. Instead, children who set goals, whatever those goals are, and work hard to achieve them tend to be the most successful. As Dr. Elkind says, "Being competitive with others is not the best trait for success."

We shouldn't shield our children from competition. To teach our children to compete with themselves and to cooperate with others would be a better approach. If children learn to compete with themselves, they will constantly push themselves to do better than they did in the past, which is the healthiest way to teach our children to reach their potential.

One mother recently told me that she used to push her nine-year-old son, Michael, to get As after she became friends with a woman whose son was one of the brightest in the class. There was only one problem: Michael had never been an A student, no matter how hard he studied.

"I was totally caught up in the competitive bullshit that goes on among friends," the mother said. "I felt that if Michael didn't do as well in school as our friend's child, then he somehow wasn't as great a kid. It got to the point that I put so much competitive pressure on Michael that he started to wheeze whenever he had to take a test or bring home his report card."

The family's pediatrician accurately diagnosed that the pressure on Michael to achieve beyond his capabilities was causing stress-induced asthma. "When the doctor told me what he thought the problem was, it hit me like a ton of bricks," Michael's mother says. "I realized that the problem was with me, not with him. He was working as hard as he could. Now, I don't worry about what other children are doing. I encourage Michael to try to beat his last score, to see how well he can do, kind of make a game out of it. And you know what? His grades have actually improved some and he hasn't had any more asthma attacks!"

Academic competition is inevitable at some time in every child's life. However, if we start teaching them early on to compete with themselves, they will be prepared to work hard and be all they can be, to paraphrase an old U.S. Army slogan. That perspective should help minimize their stress and maximize their academic performance.

Teach Them to Learn

Children who love to learn will do better in school. They will find studying less of a chore and will probably set higher academic goals for themselves. Fortunately, we can teach our children to have a love of learning and a thirst for knowledge. In fact, learning to love learning is undoubtedly the most important thing we can teach them during their academic careers.

If we want to teach our children to learn, we have to set an example by being interested learners ourselves. When we read books and newspapers, follow politics and science, or discuss issues and current events around the dinner table, we show our children that we are interested in the world around us. We also demonstrate that the learning process does not stop once we are out of school.

Teaching children to learn also means that we must be more interested in what they know than in what grade they bring home on a report card. This task is not easy, nor should we just accept our children performing poorly in school. But as Dr. Elkind says, "When we show that we're interested in what our children know, they won't get so caught up in the grades. They'll probably get good grades anyway, but they'll also be focused on the learning, the knowing and the curiosity, which is the important thing. Parents get so caught up with grades that what kids learn becomes secondary."[22]

If we teach our children to be lifelong learners,

we'll show them the way to succeed in life, as well as in their academic careers. For as the character Morpheus said in the movie *The Matrix,* "We can show them the door; they're the ones who have to walk through it."[23]

Keep Them Awake

Unfortunately, too many children are sleepwalking through that door! By the time a child finishes after-school activities, evening sports practices and games, and a quick dinner, it is often late in the evening before he can sit down to do his homework. He may even have swimming or an academic tutor early the next morning. That studies have shown 20 percent of teens falling asleep in their first two hours of school is no surprise.

Sleep requirements vary from person to person, but the average school-age child needs about ten hours of sleep a night, while the average teen requires approximately forty-five minutes less than that. How many of us can honestly say our children get that much sleep? Probably not many, yet we expect them to function optimally during the school day, absorbing information and regurgitating it with a clarity of thought that is impossible in a haze of sleep deprivation.

One study found that 51 percent of children (ages ten to eighteen) go to bed at 10:00 P.M. or later on school nights; 84 percent of children get up at 7:00 A.M. or earlier on school days; 36 percent of parents say getting their children to bed at night and waking them up in the morning is hard.[24]

Why are many of our children living in a twilight

zone? Many of us are pushing our children too hard, making sleep a casualty in the competitive battle for academic superiority. However, lack of sleep is only part of the story. Our children's biological clocks are also to blame. Their brains are programmed to stay awake until around 11:00 P.M. and to stay asleep until about 8:00 A.M. This sleep cycle is hard to change. Yet change is what we expect. Our children's daily schedules are at odds with this built-in sleep cycle. Instead of waking up at 8:00 A.M., most children must wake up before 7:00 A.M. (and sometimes long before that) because their school day begins between 7:00 and 8:00 A.M.; children may want to stay up to 11:00 P.M., but we try to force them to sleep before they are ready. In this arbitrary schedule, convenience is expected to vanquish biology. However, hundreds of thousands of years of evolution cannot be suppressed so easily.

Education writer Susan Black says, "[Children are] caught in a time warp which they can't control. Their body chemistry forces them to stay awake late at night, and their school schedules and other obligations which they have to meet force them to get up before the time when they have gotten their full quota of sleep."[25]

Black quotes one high school senior who describes the ongoing battle between the biological clock and the alarm clock. "I get out of school at 2:30 P.M., check in with my school newspaper advisor, rush to soccer practice, grab a bite to eat, work from 6:30 to 9:00 P.M., and then do homework and study until almost midnight," says the student. "I'm lucky to get six hours of sleep on school nights."

Wouldn't it be better to alter our childrens' school schedules to match their biological clocks rather than turning them into zombies? That change would allow them the sleep they need so their minds can function optimally and retain the information they receive in the classroom. Indeed, the schedule shift could help prevent a multitude of problems. Sleep-deprived children suffer from more than just lower grades. They may also suffer from a condition that experts call "pathological alertness," in which children can have troubled relationships and depression. Exhausted kids are also more likely to use drugs and alcohol, have fatal car accidents, and commit suicide. In that sense, we may literally be working our school-aged children to death.

The Minnesota Medical Association sees sleep-deprivation as a major health hazard for our children. In 1994, it sent letters to every school superintendent in the state, urging them to begin their school day later in the morning to match students' biological clocks. Many did, with tremendous results. After one high school pushed its starting time later, to 8:40 A.M., researchers found that ". . . few students fell asleep at their desks. Teachers reported students were more alert in class and much more engaged in class discussions. Students got better grades on schoolwork and [were in] a better mood more of the time. Parents said their children were 'easier to live with.' There was also time in the morning to talk with their children. And participation in after-school activities remained the same."[26]

Instituting changes like this is hard, requiring a coordinated effort by concerned parents in each community to educate school superintendents, teachers, school board representatives and other parents. However, many of us have put at least as much effort into making our children academic superstars. If we pay attention to our children's biological clocks, our efforts may be more likely to succeed, helping to give our children a sense of stability within their own home.

In the meantime, there are ways to try to keep your child from becoming sleep-deprived.

- Don't let your child play computer games or do other "stimulating" activities before she goes to bed.
- Don't let her drink caffeine at night.
- Give her time to wind down before bed.
- Try to have her go to sleep at the same time each night and wake up at the same time each morning, even on weekends.
- Exposing her to bright lights in the morning and limiting exposure to light at night can help reset your child's sleep-wake cycle.

Homework Should Be Reasonable

I was shocked when, a few years ago, a friend of mine told me his son brought home an hour's worth of homework. The child was only in kindergarten. I didn't think about it at the time, but what I should have been most shocked about was the fact that my friend was bragging about his five-year-old son's homework!

Homework is essential to reinforce and augment what a child learns in the classroom, but Americans have begun to equate the quantity of their children's homework with the quality of their education. If such a correlation were valid, our children should know more than ever before because teachers are piling on the work, even for children in grade school. A recent University of Michigan study found that while children aged six to eight spent an average of forty-four minutes a week doing homework in 1981, they spent more than two hours a week in 1997. "Definitely, there is more homework," says one professor of education. "Children today are doing more homework in the elementary grades than they did ten years ago."[27, 28]

The problem is that our children's academic performance has not improved, despite this barrage of homework. Some studies have shown that homework can raise middle school and high school students' grades, but the pressure for academic success has been pushed onto our youngest students, and no evidence supports the notion that homework helps them. One University of Missouri study showed no correlation between the amount of homework a child has in elementary school and his chances for future academic success.[29] Other studies indicate that homework in grades K-5 may harm a child's attitude toward school.[30]

Too much homework may also lead to burnout, no matter how old the child. "I could have five hours of homework a night, but I have to choose what to do, because there's no way I can do it all," said one high school student. Another adds, "Caffeine is huge. It gets you through the five hours of homework."[31]

How can our children perform their best when they're buried under a mountain of homework, extracurricular activities and athletic events? With so little time to delve deeply into the subjects they're studying, is it surprising that the performance of American children lags behind many other children around the world?

"I'm up to all hours doing my homework," said one

Massachusetts senior. "You feel like you're going to have a nervous breakdown before college."

This trend has led some experts to recommend doing away with homework altogether. In her book *The End of Homework: How Homework Disrupts Families, Overburdens Children, and Limits Learning,* Etta Kralovec argues that too much homework makes our kids less motivated and causes them to perform poorly in school. She says parents and schools are misguided if they think more homework will lead to higher scores on the standardized tests that most colleges use as part of their application screening process.

However, eliminating homework is not the answer; assigning a reasonable amount is. Colorado educator Aileen Dickey says a general rule of thumb is that a child should have approximately ten minutes of homework a night for each year he's been in school; a first-grader should have ten minutes of homework; a sixth-grader, an hour; a high school senior, two hours. These amounts are a far cry from what goes on in many schools around the country, and the problem is made worse by the way many of us overschedule our kids. We run them ragged, then expect them to ace their homework assignments.

"Scheduling would be the first thing I'd look at," said Bruce Knight, principal of McKelvey Elementary School in Missouri. He thinks homework would be less of a burden if we didn't push our children so hard in their extracurricular activities.

But a national group of parents and educators, called Parents United for Sane Homework, or PUSH, is convinced that too much homework is, indeed, a major factor in turning our schools into a cyclone of stress. The group says, ". . . the current 'pile on the

homework' ethic in elementary school is wrong-
headed and harmful to our children."

The members of "PUSH" believe

- Homework should be minimized, not maximized.
- "Family Connection Activities," "Curriculum
  Completion Activities" or unstructured play are
  of far more value than homework.
- Homework should be individualized.
- We should do what is appropriate for our chil-
  dren now, not "prepare for the future."[32]

One Indiana school district has begun implementing some of these ideas in an attempt to keep their
elementary school kids from burning out. A new
East Porter County school district policy states,
"Assignments which consistently require that most
of each evening be devoted to homework preparation are inappropriate."

Roger Luekens, superintendent at East Porter,
said the new policy encourages homework that
"enriches, reinforces, prepares and gives students
skills." Homework given for the purposes of busy-
work is discouraged.[33]

As with school starting times, changing homework
policies will require the concerted effort of parents
who are worried about their children's stress levels.
Unfortunately, this change may prove difficult given
the number of parents who are caught up in the "more
is better" mentality that is so typical of the baby boom
generation. In the meantime, you can lower your
child's stress by encouraging her to do her best, helping her wherever possible and by not packing her
after-school schedules so tightly that she is exhausted
by the time she sits down to do her assignments.

Gifted Programs Are Not Always Gifts

How many times have you heard parents brag that their child is in a gifted program in their school? In our competitive society, acceptance to a gifted program is often seen as the first step on the road to the Ivy League (or other distinguished universities), one that many parents insist their child take. I have even heard of parents who have nearly come to blows with elementary school administrators upon learning that their child didn't qualify for admission to a gifted program.

However, Dr. Sal Severe believes gifted programs may be trouble at younger ages. He says, "If your kid qualifies for an advanced program, that's great, but I always tell them to look carefully at the program. If it's the kind of program that teaches kids creative problem solving and alternative ways to think, that's good. But if it's just going to be more intense academics, in third grade they don't need that. I find in those more intense programs, by seventh or eighth grade a lot of these kids are burning out. Kids who get in early are often the first ones to drop out. They just kind of see it as extra work, and for what?"

Dr. Severe points out that gifted programs do matter in high school; the advanced courses are meaningful and can help a child gain acceptance into college. Parents should be wary, though, of exposing their children to intensely academic programs when they are very young. Dr. Severe says it's hard to put academics into perspective, even for him; he has a daughter in elementary school. "I mean, the stuff she learns in first grade, is it important? Sure. But is it going to affect the way she lives the rest of her life? I don't know. I just want her to have a good attitude about school. And I think that we sometimes just forget that, especially in the primary grades.

"Kids are maybe more capable than we thought they were, but still they're just kids."[34]

A gifted program is truly a gift if it cultivates a child's creativity instead of just giving him more of what he already receives in the classroom.

Have Some Perspective

Assistant Principal Aileen Dickey says, "It would be nice if parents recognized that elementary school is the practice, it's not the race. I think we confuse that an awful lot. It's not the race. . . . It's the preparation for the race."[35]

Many of us forget that our child's performance in elementary school, or even middle school, will not determine what college he attends. However, the pressure we put on him to perform early in his academic career may well affect his attitude toward school and learning. Our efforts to help him win the race may make him crash and burn before he even finishes his first lap.

And if, after all this, you are still having trouble putting early academic achievement in the proper perspective, check out the following list of academic "failures."

- Einstein was four years old before he could speak.
- Isaac Newton did poorly in grade school and was considered "unpromising."
- Beethoven's music teacher once said of him, "As a composer, he is hopeless."

- When Thomas Edison was a youngster, his teacher told him he was too stupid to learn anything.
- Winston Churchill had to repeat the sixth grade because he did not complete the tests that were required for promotion.[36]

Most of us want our child to be the smartest, the best student, or the class valedictorian. But success manifests itself in different ways. If we keep academic achievement in the proper perspective, our children will benefit much more than if we turn school into a source of stress and instability. The solution is academic!

NINE

TAKING THE FUN
OUT OF THE GAMES

J immy stood at the free throw line and waited for the referee to toss him the ball. He looked at the scoreboard: two seconds left, his team down by one point.

"Come on, Jimmy. Nice and easy, just like we practiced." He looked over to the sidelines and saw his father yelling to him and pushing his hand upward in a mock basketball shot. At the same time, he felt a gnawing stomach pain and nausea begin to overwhelm him.

Jimmy had complained of stomach pain and nausea almost every day for two years, but the symptoms became a lot worse whenever he stepped onto the basketball court. His father had been a star basketball player in high school and had tried to groom Jimmy to follow in his footsteps. But no matter how hard he tried or how many hours his dad spent drilling him on how to dribble and shoot, Jimmy just didn't have "it." He would never be a star basketball player. In fact, he didn't really want to be a basketball player at all. He was much more interested in reading and writing. He just didn't want to disappoint his dad.

The referee finally tossed him the ball. Jimmy stood with his toes on the free throw line and bounced the ball once, twice, a third time. The stomachache grew worse with each dribble. Jimmy knew that if he missed, he would have to endure his father's lectures for days to come. Embarrassing his dad would hurt far more than merely losing a basketball game.

Jimmy looked up at the rim and pushed the ball up with all his might. The ball arced upward before descending toward the hoop. For a moment, Jimmy thought he was going to make his father proud. But as the ball careened off the back of the rim, Jimmy looked to the sidelines in time to see his dad kick the bleachers in anger. At that moment, Jimmy swore to himself that he would never play basketball again.

Jimmy's story is not unique. I have heard stories like his from colleagues around the country who practice in a variety of medical specialties. When the fun is taken out of games, many kids end up with headaches, stomachaches, muscle pains, joint aches, nervous itches and twitches, eating disorders, depression, temper tantrums and other psychological problems.

Youth sports are supposed to make our children happy and physically fit, not maladjusted and sick!

No wonder so many kids like Jimmy drop out of athletics long before they become adults. In one survey of kids between the ages of eleven and eighteen who were involved in organized sports, researchers found that 35 percent of them planned to stop playing the next year. In fact, 73 percent of children quit playing sports by age thirteen. The two most common reasons children drop out of sports, according to a study by the Youth Sports Institute at Michigan State University, are that the kids lost interest in the sport or they aren't having fun playing it anymore.[1] A pretty sorry statement, indeed.

To be sure, some kids drop out of sports as part of a normal process of growing up, maturing and deciding what they like and dislike. Choices have to be made about time commitments; most children, like most adults, tend to choose to spend their time on activities they do well. But for too many kids, dropping out of sports is not a decision but a necessity. They're burned out, sick and tired of trying to force their children's games to meet adult expectations.

Good Sports

Organized sports can teach important lessons about competition and winning and losing gracefully, lessons that can reach beyond the playing field. One high school sports administrator pointed this out in a recent National Federation of High School Associations' bulletin: "Sportsmanship is the starting point, if not the essence, of good citizenship. It is what we're supposed to teach in educational athletics more than anything else."

Sports can also build a child's self-esteem. Some research has even shown that kids who participate in sports and have more organized lives tend to earn better grades in school.

"The research we've done shows that 95 percent of the things that go on in youth sports are positive," says Dr. Maureen Weiss, an education professor at the University of Virginia. "Only about 5 percent are negative. But there are about twenty million kids participating in youth sports. Even 5 percent of that number means that at least a million kids are influenced negatively by sports."

Unfortunately, Dr. Weiss told me, it's the parents who often spoil the fun. "We find that when children feel their parents are positive and supportive, their

motivation to continue [playing sports] is high."
When they don't, kids often choose to tune out, turn
off and drop out. Not surprisingly, Dr. Weiss's
research has found that parents and kids can see
things very differently. When parents think they're
being supportive, children often think they're being
pressured to perform; when parents believe their
actions show approval, kids often perceive disap-
proval. When children think they're being pressured
or their parents disapprove of their performance,
they suffer "competitive stress, interpersonal stress
within their team," and they stop playing sports.

Whose Dream Is It, Anyway?

I love baseball movies, and one of my favorites is
Field of Dreams, starring Kevin Costner. In the film,
Costner plays Ray Kinsella, who hears a voice whis-
pering to him while he stands in his cornfield: "If you
build it, he will come." He follows this suggestion
and builds a baseball diamond in the middle of his
cornfield. But an irony is present: baseball had
driven a wedge between Kinsella and his late father.
"He never made it as a ballplayer, so he tried to get
his son to make it for him," Kinsella says. "By the
time I was ten, playing baseball got to be like eating
vegetables or taking out the garbage. So when I was
fourteen, I started to refuse. Can you believe that?
An American boy refusing to have a catch with his
father?"

Kinsella eventually built his "field of dreams" and
was able to have an imaginary catch with his father
without feeling any of the pressures he felt when he
was young. If only life were so easy! Unfortunately,

for most children whose parents burn them out on sports, the Hollywood ending doesn't usually happen.

World-renowned psychologist Carl Jung said, "The greatest burden a child must bear is the unlived life of its parents." Dr. Jung never saw *Field of Dreams,* and he was not referring specifically to unfulfilled dreams of athletic stardom, but nowhere is his statement exemplified better than in what *Time* magazine recently referred to as the "crazy culture of kids' sports."[2]

Many people can point to friends and acquaintances as examples. The craziness can start innocently enough. For example, a friend of mine who played second string on the football team at a small college outfitted his newborn boy with a baby-sized New York Giants football jersey and put a miniature football in his crib. Now that the child is five, my friend constantly brags to anyone who will listen about how gifted an athlete his son is.

Will my friend's son grow up to be a professional football player? It's possible, but unlikely. Will he want to? That question is even more relevant, but it will probably never be asked. Answering "no" to the question would undoubtedly disappoint his father.

Falling into that trap is easy. I played basketball in school and would love it if my son, Jacob, also played it. At six years old, he loves shooting baskets with me on his little adjustable hoop. Of course, I'm probably more into him playing basketball than he is, and to just play with him and not coach him on his shooting or dribbling techniques takes a tremendous effort. Sometimes my restraint fails me and I end up making our play time seem more like a basketball drill than a game. When that happens, Jacob usually loses interest and tells me he doesn't want to play anymore. The only thing I succeeded in doing was taking the fun out of our game and potentially turning him off to the sport that I love.

One woman I spoke to has her own way of avoiding this pitfall. Jean's a pretty mean tennis player, but she won't bring her six-year-old daughter to the court with her when she plays. She doesn't want to pressure her child to play tennis. If the girl shows interest as she grows older, however, Jean will bring her daughter to the courts and introduce her to the game slowly. Jean feels that in this way she won't fall prey to the error of trying to live vicariously through her child, and burning her out in the process.

Sometimes parents either don't see the signs their children are burning out, or we see them but don't want to accept them. I frequently confront this problem in my medical practice. Eight-year-old Michael was one of these burned-out children. He had throbbing headaches almost every day for a year and had been to see a half-dozen doctors in an attempt to find out the cause. Michael was subjected to blood tests, CAT scans, brain wave tests and a spinal tap; his doctors found nothing and eventually put him on daily medication to prevent his headaches.

The one thing Michael's doctors neglected to explore was his psychosocial well-being. Such an investigation is an important part of any workup for a chronic condition, especially in children, and only when I began to ask Michael about his activities and what he liked to do did I uncover the cause of his headaches. Michael's father had been a competitive swimmer when he was in high school and college and he wanted Michael to follow in his wake. Michael learned to swim when he was four years old, and since then, his father had trained him. The only problem was that Michael didn't like swimming.

"I don't want to be a swimmer. I don't even like the water," Michael told his father, but the comments fell on deaf ears.

"Don't worry. You'll get to like it. Once you start winning some races, you'll love it. I promise," his father said. For the previous year, beginning at approximately the same time that his headaches had started, Michael had to wake up at 5:00 A.M. in order to practice swimming before school started.

A number of visits passed before Michael's parents were convinced that his headaches were related to swimming. After some heavy soul-searching, they eventually asked Michael if he wanted to be a swimmer. I wasn't sure whether Michael would have the guts to tell them the truth, knowing that he would probably disappoint his father. However, when he told them, "No, I don't want to be a swimmer," I could see a sense of relief in his face. Within days of stopping his swimming routine, Michael's headaches also stopped.

We parents can love our kids, nurture them, guide them and strive to be role models, but we can't live vicariously through them. Our kids need to live their own lives, find their own way and follow their own dreams. After all, it's not us out there on the playing field or the wrestling mat, on the tennis court or in the pool. We can celebrate with them when they succeed and be there for them when they fail, but too many of us see our children's athletic performance as a measure of how successful we are as parents.

How many times have you seen a parent puff out his or her chest when a child gets a hit or wins a race? There's a fine line between the pride of saying, "That's my boy," and the braggadocio that says, in effect, "My child's a star, so that means I'm a great parent."

Dr. Thomas Tutko, a psychology professor at San Jose State University and expert on sports psychology, has said, "I think the key happens to be that parents, without being aware of it, are really seeing the child as a reflection of their child-rearing habits. So if little Charlie does well, it shows we're a great family. If little Charlie is a star, that means that we as parents have done a magnificent job. Whether or not they're aware of it, slowly but surely, they become involved in the performance because it is a reflection on them as individuals."[3]

One man told me how he avoids this situation when he's in the stands at his son's Little League games: he makes a point of clapping and saying something positive when children from both teams come to bat or make a play on the field. It doesn't matter whether the child strikes out or makes an error; he claps regardless. This unconditional approval is his way of supporting his son, demonstrating good sportsmanship and reminding himself that the games are about kids having fun, not parental pride.

Unrealistic Expectations

A few weeks before I wrote this chapter, tennis sensation Venus Williams beat her sister Serena in the semifinals at Wimbledon, on the way to winning her first Wimbledon tennis championship. The Williams sisters' tennis success is the product of years of planning on the part of their father, Richard Williams. He started them on their path to stardom almost as soon as they were able to walk. Although he pushed his daughters hard, as many so-called "tennis parents" do, he also knew when to stop pushing. In fact, some people called him foolish and inept when he refused to allow the girls, then ages nine and ten, to play in more junior tournaments. But Richard Williams didn't want to wear his girls out. He had seen too many young "phenoms" burned out by the grueling tennis circuit. He wasn't going to let that happen to Venus and Serena.

Richard Williams was lucky. His daughters' physical, mental and emotional abilities lived up to his expectations. Yet for every Venus or Serena Williams, thousands of other children will never be elite athletes no matter how hard they try, or how hard their parents push them. The failure to live up to a parent's expectations can have devastating psychological and physical consequences.

Dr. Joel Fish, director of the Center for Sports Psychology in Philadelphia, tells the story of a ten-year-old girl who had stopped eating. She felt that she didn't "deserve" food because she wasn't performing well in her track meets. Apparently, her times had not improved as she and her coach had hoped.

"Her parents didn't ask if she had done her best," Dr. Fish says. "Rather, they expressed great disappointment in her. As a result, she lost confidence in herself and in her abilities. She began to think of herself as 'not good enough' . . . this girl's self-esteem had vanished, and she was only ten."[4]

This girl's signs of burnout were more dramatic than the symptoms most children exhibit, but when we set unrealistic expectations for our kids, we set them up for failure. As we push our children to compete at an earlier age, these expectations become an even greater problem. One study by the National Youth Sports Coaches Association found that virtually half of five- to eight-year-olds surveyed didn't have the skills to play in the sports in which their parents enrolled them.[5] We may think it's cute to see our young children kick a ball or swing a bat, but when they don't possess the skills to do so effectively, what looks cute to us can very easily turn into frustration and humiliation for them.

Some parents try to combat this situation by hiring private coaches for their children. I know a number of children whose parents hired a private baseball coach to teach them how to play when they were still very young. After a few years of private lessons, these kids can certainly hit and field well, but many of them are already beginning to show signs of burning out, and one has already quit the sport that his parents had groomed him to play.

I don't know about you, but when I was growing up, my dad taught me how to catch and throw, hit and field. More than that, the time I spent with him was "our time." Sports helped cement our relationship, even when it was strained by all the normal issues that distance growing sons from their fathers and vice versa. I always looked forward to playing ball with my dad.

A man named Paul told me that he tries to pass this father-son experience on to his own son by setting aside one day a week (in the spring and summer) in which he leaves work an hour early and takes his seven-year-old son to the park. His son chooses which game they'll play that day, and the two of them spend an hour or two just tossing a baseball or football, throwing a Frisbee, or sometimes just riding bicycles together. The sport doesn't matter; the time together does.

Winning and Losing

"I'm sitting at the scorekeeper's table dutifully keeping score for my son's Little League game," says Louveda Morris. "As I'm doing this, I'm listening to a pair of dads discussing the game. They are angry at their team's performance. What struck me was not so much that they were angry, although this is what initially caught my attention, but that they were parents from the winning team!

"Now I can understand being upset with your child if he were goofing off and not contributing to the team. But these men were angry because of some errors the team made that allowed a few runs for our team."

All I can say to Louveda is welcome to the world of youth sports. Legendary football coach Knute Rockne once said, "Show me a gracious loser and I'll show you a loser." Many of today's parents live by this philosophy, but I doubt whether even Knute Rockne himself would have applied it to ten-year-olds playing organized football.

The win-at-all-costs, ultracompetitive attitude that many parents promote is evident in the increasingly aggressive and unsportsmanlike behavior seen at children's sporting events around the country.

- In Florida, a Little League player was hit in the head with a bat and adults brawled with each other after coaches from both teams traded insults.

- A midget football game in Pennsylvania turned into a free-for-all that involved fifty players and spectators.
- A father was beaten to death by another father during a youth hockey game in Massachusetts. The attack occurred in front of the young hockey players including the man's sons.
- The National Association of Sports Officials in Racine, Wisconsin, receives two or three calls a week from officials assaulted by an angry parent or spectator, according to spokesman Bob Still.
- One father was so unhappy about the treatment his son received from referees that he sharpened the buckle on his son's football helmet. The buckle, acting like a razor, gashed five players on the opposing team. One player's laceration was so severe that he required twelve stitches.

"There's a definite trend toward more violence and more pressure on the game officials," said Ron Allen, an assistant commissioner with the Florida High School Activities Association. "I'm talking about players, I'm talking about parents and spectators."[6]

"At local ball fields, parents are getting out of control. Winning is everything," Florida State Representative Eleanor Sobel (D-Hollywood) said after a game turned to violence in her home district. "The psychological impact on the kids is not good."[7]

With role models like these, no wonder some children have become competitive to a fault. Dr. Randy Weeks, a neuropsychologist who treats many children who suffer from burnout, says that parents who have a win-at-all-costs mentality transmit this killer instinct to their children. The result is a volatile combination of youthful energy, high intensity and hyper-competitiveness, mixed with emotional immaturity. "They need not only to win, but to be ahead, to put their foot in somebody's face to be on top. It's not like competition. It's competition with anger," he said.

This intensity can be particularly damaging when championships are on the line. One study found that in youth hockey tournaments, players get hurt four to six times more often during play-offs than in the regular season.[8] The reasons: more body checking and more intense play.

Dr. Charles Tator, professor of neurosurgery at the University of Toronto, says this study provides hard evidence that the win-at-all-costs attitude needs to be changed. "I think it is symptomatic of this injury problem that winning is inordinately more important than attention to safety and respect for the opponents.

"The leagues, the coaches, the parents, the referees, the players are not paying sufficient attention to safety, and they're paying too much attention to winning and 'killing the opponents,'" Tator says.[9]

The facts back up Dr. Tator: more than 775,000 kids between the ages of five and fourteen are treated in hospital emergency rooms for sports-related injuries each year.[10] Millions more are treated in doctors' offices, physical therapy departments or at home by Dr. Mom. I've seen Little League baseball players as young as ten going out on the pitcher's mound, throwing curve balls by twisting their arms, then plunging their elbows into bags of ice when the game is over. Four or five days later, they do it again. It's bad enough coaches are not worried about the potential damage caused to growing tendons and bones, but what about the kids' parents?

Let's face it, many parents and coaches have lost perspective. How else can we explain the results of a recent study by the Minnesota Amateur Sports Commission? This group found that almost half of the children who played sports said they had been called names, yelled at or insulted; 21 percent had been pressured to play with an injury; 17.5 percent said they had been hit, kicked or slapped; almost 10 percent said they had been pressured to purposely hurt an opposition player.[11] According to Fred Engh, president of the National Alliance for Youth Sports, these results indicate that, in some cases, parents' obsession with winning has created a climate of athletic child abuse.[12]

One athletic association in Jupiter, Florida, is using a novel way to make parents behave themselves: they have to attend a mandatory sportsmanship class and sign a code of ethics that commits them to setting a good example for their children. If parents don't sign, their children don't play.

Other communities have followed suit. In Michigan, a seminar focusing on good sportsmanship sold out after drawing two thousand parents, coaches and athletic directors. In Cambridge, Massachusetts, the youth soccer league asked parents and other spectators not to cheer or yell instructions during matches. In Ohio, a soccer league started what they call "Silent Sunday," where parents are not supposed to cheer or jeer the kids on the playing field; leagues in Maryland and Connecticut have done the same on their "Silent Saturdays."

Some sports officials in Ohio, California and Florida think the situation has become so bad that they've even toyed with the idea of having spectator-free games. In a Rye Brook, New York, recreational basketball league, officials didn't need to ban parents from games; the kids did. Before the league's postseason three-on-three tournament began, league officials asked the kids whether they wanted their parents to be allowed to watch the tournament. The answer: a resounding "no!"

A No-Win (or Lose) Situation

Losing is no fun, and if you're a young child whose self-image and self-esteem aren't fully developed, losing is *really* no fun. I can remember watching kids from other teams getting large championship trophies at the end of the season while my team left empty-handed; the experience was tough. I was fortunate, though, to have been one of the kids who was picked to play a lot and often made the baseball and basketball all-star teams. That fact probably did a lot to give me the confidence that, as I grew up, allowed me to set high goals and pursue them relentlessly.

Other kids aren't as lucky. They sit on the bench wondering if, and when, they will have their chance to play. Unfortunately, many coaches, with the consent of parents looking for confirmation that their children, and by extension themselves, are "winners," will sacrifice these childrens' playing time if they think it will hurt the team's chances of winning.

Is seeing your seven-year-old holding up a championship trophy so important? The truth is that all this emphasis on winning seems to be more important to us parents than it is to our kids. Indeed, most kids just want to have fun. One study found that almost 80 percent of children would rather play for a losing team than sit on the bench for a winning team.

Some parents and youth sports directors have accepted this outlook and are trying to do something about it. They have created what I like to call a no-lose situation: a kids' sport league that does not keep track of who wins and who loses, puts an emphasis on letting all kids play, and rewards all players equally for their participation.

The largest organization to experiment with this kind of program is the Massachusetts Youth Soccer Association (MYSA). When kids under ten are playing, the MYSA doesn't keep official game scores, it doesn't keep standings and it doesn't hand out championship trophies at the end of the year. Individual leagues can either give participation awards to all players, or they can choose to give no awards at the end of the season.

Jim Gondek, executive director of the MYSA, told me they're doing it so that kids will enjoy soccer and not lose interest. And he said for most kids, championships and trophies aren't the most important things.

"They're having fun at the younger age groups and they're learning," he said with satisfaction.

The MYSA is serious about its philosophy of just letting kids have fun. It will not give permission for one of its under-ten teams to play in an out-of-state tournament if it's a results-oriented competition. They've even gone so far as to prevent one of their teams from participating in a tournament at Disney World.

Remember "the thrill of victory . . . and the agony of defeat"? In Massachusetts, young soccer players are spared these emotional highs and lows. One MYSA coach says this approach will give kids "more opportunity to develop all-around soccer smartness and enhance natural, intrinsic competition."[13]

This organization may sound very New Age to some parents. Jim Gondek admits some opposition since the MYSA changed its rules: "Some parents think we're depriving children of important life experiences and valuable lessons [such as] how to lose gracefully." Jim doesn't disagree with these parents, but he feels that lessons like winning and losing can be taught after age ten.

The MYSA is not alone in emphasizing fun instead of competition. The Calverton (Maryland) recreational league has been emphasizing fun for almost ten years. In all of their leagues involving children under fifteen years of age, there's no official scorekeeping, no one keeps track of win-loss records and everyone receives the same award at the end of the season.

David Cooley, president of the recreational league and commissioner of the soccer program, says the main objective is for all of the kids to play and have fun. At first, he told me, scoreless games were hard to sell to some parents.

"I initially used the argument that when you keep score . . . half the kids go away not feeling good. [With this program], all the kids can feel good after the games are over. It increases personal gratification for each kid."

Fourteen-year-old Davis Glasser played in the Calverton recreational league from the time he was in kindergarten. He says that even without an official scorekeeper, the kids know who wins and who loses, but it's not a big deal.

"Everyone knows what the score is, but it's good that you don't have as much pressure. Everyone knows what happens cause kids are bound to take [the games] seriously, but it's not like someone's saying, 'Your team stinks. You're in last place.' Everyone has fun."

When I asked Davis if he thought he would have learned more about winning and losing gracefully if he had played in a competitive league, he didn't hesitate to answer. "It's not a problem because you know what you've done. My teammates and I don't need a brass band [to tell us we've won] because we know what we've done and we're proud of ourselves. And we're in it together."

The proof is in the pyramid. In ordinary sports leagues, more and more kids drop out each year, so that by the age of thirteen, most have stopped playing at all. It's called a "pyramiding effect." But the MYSA says that since it instituted the noncompetitive rules, the number of children playing soccer have stayed constant.

The Calverton recreational league has more long-term experience with this no-lose situation, and the parents, kids and staff involved in the program are especially enthusiastic about its virtues.

"We have no more pyramiding effect," says David Cooley. "There are as many older kids playing in our league as younger kids. A lot of people thought the older kids wouldn't like it, but they've stayed with it. The social aspects of the game become very important.

"The parents also love it. One of the things I do [on my soccer team] is play with fewer players on each side so that the kids get more touches on the ball and more opportunities [to play]."

Playing is what joining a team is all about. Ali Murdoch is a nine-year-old girl who started playing organized sports in the Calverton soccer program. She played well enough that when she reached the second grade, her mother decided to move her to a more competitive league. That's when trouble started.

"The coach told Ali, 'You have to prove to me you deserve playing time,'" said Nancy Femiano, Ali's mother. "The kids were so tense and afraid of making mistakes. There's no way they could play well."

Ali sat on the bench most of the season, which damaged her self-esteem. "She said, 'Mom, I'm not a good soccer player, am I?'" Ali's injured ego sustained another blow when the coach took the team to an out-of-state tournament and left Ali behind.

"I didn't get to play," Ali told me. "He didn't need any more players. It felt kind of bad." Actually, according to her mother, Ali cried hard over the insult.

Nancy says these experiences caused Ali to develop behavioral problems. "She fought, [threw] temper tantrums, wouldn't follow through with anything and would just tune you out when you were talking to her." Ali's doctor recognized the relationship between her behavioral problems and the stress inflicted on her developing psyche. Not surprisingly, she recommended pulling Ali off the team.

"She's just starting on a different team with a different coach who cares more about the kids playing and having fun than winning and losing," Nancy says. "The behavioral problems are better. Ali's self-esteem is better now."

Nancy doesn't want to see her five-year-old son go through the same tribulations. He is starting in the Calverton recreational league this year, and Nancy says she's going to keep him in the noncompetitive leagues.

Chet Speiser agrees that for the younger kids, fun

is more important than competition. He was an accomplished baseball player in his youth, but he's totally committed to the Calverton philosophy. "Seventy-five to 85 percent of kids playing [in our program] come from other communities. Many of the parents have told me, '[My child] wasn't learning anything [in the other program]. He's not that good but here he's playing and learning now.'

"But the athletic kids like our program, too. My grandson's been recruited by a number of eleven-year-old "elite" baseball teams, but he doesn't want to play for them. He enjoys playing in the recreational league because he has fun."

Putting the Fun Back in Games

Some of you are probably shaking your heads right now and thinking that a sports league without standings or scores is too unreal. After all, real life, at least the way we live it, is about competition and winning or losing: who has a better job, more money, a higher IQ or a bigger house. Or more athletic children. That outlook has always been my instinct, too; I'm as competitive as the next person (my family and friends would say more so!). But if we stopped to recognize the unhealthy effects of living our lives in the rat race, we would see the value in reconsidering our basic assumptions, at least when our children are involved. If we want our kids to reap the benefits of participating in sports, we need to make sure we don't burn them out or turn them off in the process.

My *Random House College Dictionary* defines the word "game" as "an amusement or pastime:

children's games." Notice that we refer to basketball *games,* baseball *games* and football *games.* Sure, hockey and tennis players play matches and golfers play tournaments, but we still ask people who play these sports, "How's your *game?*" In fact, boxing is the only sport I can think of where the word "game" isn't used in some way when talking about it. Why? Probably because there's nothing fun about getting hit in the head repeatedly, and games are supposed to be about being amused and having fun!

This chapter is not meant to be an indictment of organized sports for kids. I played sports growing up; my children are involved in them right now. Sports can and should be a fun and positive influence in our kids' lives. We just need to be careful not to ruin it for them. So if you want to put the fun back into games, here are some ways to do it.

1. *Ask yourself if your child is interested in sports in the first place.* The question sounds obvious, but it's easy to ignore. When my son was four years old, I kept trying to get him to shoot baskets on his plastic hoop. When he showed no interest, I started to worry that he wouldn't be interested in the sport I love. I forced myself to back off, and then to my surprise, by the time he was five, I had to pull the basketball out of his arms each day and drag him into the house for dinner! The moral is, that you can't force a kid to be interested in anything, including sports, and you shouldn't even try. If they're ready and willing, you'll know it.

2. *Don't make unrealistic expectations or set unrealistic goals.* Tiger Woods is one of the greatest golfers ever. And while it's true that his parents

exposed him to the game when he was only ten months old, they did not pressure him to play.[14] He showed an unusual amount of interest in the game on his own, even when he was very young. But let's be honest, no matter how early you start, chances are your son won't be another Tiger Woods, nor will your daughter be another Venus Williams. Former pro baseball player Jim Sundberg says, "A lot of parents in sports think that if they manage and plan and program everything for some kind of end result, their child will be a star and everything will turn out just great."[15] But he says that's not likely to happen. And I would add that if you have delusions of your child's future grandeur, the only thing you'll likely end up with is a kid who feels he or she is a failure or a disappointment.

3. *After a game, try asking your child if he had fun before you talk about his performance.* Neuropsychologist Dr. Steven Baskin told me the story of his son, Sam, who was an all-star Little League player. If Steve couldn't attend one of his games, his tendency as a parent was to ask straight out, "Did you get any hits? Did you win?" But he says he found out that if he asked his son, "Did you have a good time?" his child responded much better to it. "If I said, 'Did you have fun?' he'd talk about it and have a good time. Every time I asked him 'How'd you do?' he'd get much quieter. He doesn't like that. He's a kid. He wants to have fun."

4. *Instead of hiring a private coach, go outside and play with your child yourself.* Even if you're not an athlete, in the long run your child will get

more out of spending time with you than doing drills with a coach.

5. *When you're playing sports with them at home, focus on the element of play.* Don't get hung up on keeping score or making rules. Keep it fun.

6. *Encourage your child to play nonorganized or pickup games in the neighborhood or at a local park.* Those games are often the most fun. They're also often the games children get the most out of. "We were continually organizing one game or another," writes astronaut Edwin "Buzz" Aldrin, the second man to walk on the moon. "In those days there were no structured athletic teams for youngsters. I think we learned a good deal more by doing it for ourselves than we would have if there had been a Little League or any other kind of structured organization. Doing it for ourselves helped develop leadership abilities and the kind of competitive spirit that I would eventually discover characterizes so much of later life."[16] No one can call "Buzz" an underachiever, and he did it all without playing organized sports, or receiving private coaching lessons!

I heard about one woman in California who wanted to put the fun back in her son's games. She was tired of the arguing and poor sportsmanship in her son's ice hockey league so she decided to organize a street hockey game for him on the cul-de-sac in front of their house. She called a number of her son's classmates and invited them for an informal game each weekend. The kids had so much fun that they played almost every weekend for almost two years. I was told that all of them enjoyed their neighborhood games much more than their ice hockey games because they didn't have to worry about winning or pleasing their coaches.

7. *If your child plays in an organized league, make sure it has a policy of making sure all players play in every game.* As one child said to me so colorfully: "Riding pine sucks!"

8. *If it's available, consider a nonscoring league like the one in Calverton, Maryland.* This guideline is especially true for younger children.

9. *Make sure your child is physically capable of handling the physical stresses of the sport he or she plays.* If your child is small for his age, Pop Warner football may not be the best choice. If he's throwing a pitch that requires him to ice his arm after each game, make him stop.

10. *Don't let your child play hurt.* He may beg and plead, but your job as a parent is to look out for his best interests. No childhood contest is so important that it's worth the risk of turning a minor injury into a major one that can affect his future physical condition.

11. *Even if your child doesn't make the high school team, you should encourage her to play the sport she loves.* Remind her of the fun she has playing the games and, if necessary, help her to find time to play with family and friends. If she stays connected to a sport she loves, she can remain physically active when she becomes an adult.

12. *Remember that the game is for kids, not for adults.* No matter how badly you want to be out on the field, you can't be. So sit back and enjoy the fact that you and your child have something

in common. Heaven knows, that connection may not last for long!

13. *Praise your child's effort, even if he fails.* The encouragement will keep him going and will probably help his performance. Besides, he already knows if he lost or played poorly. He doesn't need you to point it out.

14. *Talk to your kid's coach.* Make sure he agrees with you that fun and safety are as important as winning. Also, you should discuss his philosophy on doling out playing time to his players. Nancy Femiano and a number of her fellow parents did just that before letting their children play on their new soccer team. The parents banded together to tell the coach that they wanted all the children to get playing time, they didn't want the team to play in tournaments unless all the children were allowed to go and they didn't want competition to overshadow their childrens' fun. Nancy says that if a coach doesn't agree to these demands, parents should pull their kids off the team and search for another coach, or if necessary, another league.

15. *Set a good example. Demonstrating pride when your child performs well is great, but remember that you're proud of your child, not yourself.* Despite what we may want to believe, we have very little to do with how well our child performs on the field or the balance beam. Setting a good example also means being a good sport. It's sometimes tempting to yell "Four eyes!" at an umpire, but when we behave like that, we send a message to our kids that it's not how you play the game that's important, but whether you win or lose. That outlook may have been

good enough for Coach Knute Rockne and his football teams, but as good parents we should set our standards higher.

PART III

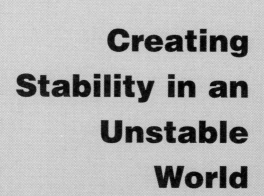

Creating
Stability in an
Unstable
World

TEN

STRESS MANAGEMENT 101

I've seen the numbers of stressed-out children increase over the last several years," writes Judy, a school nurse in Texas. "Stress presents itself in many ways: stomachaches, headaches, inability to concentrate, irritability, etc. Many parents today are overachievers idealistically, meaning they expect more of their children than of themselves I, too, am guilty of the same thing.

"I recently lost my seventeen-year-old son in an automobile accident. He was rushing to get to school when he lost control of his car and hit a tree. He was to have played in an orchestra competition that day and was in the middle of studying for exams. Clint was stressed, rushed and late. 'If only I had . . .' are the words that haunt me to this very day.

"Through my self-imposed guilt and sorrow I have tried to find answers as to what I might learn from this experience. One of them has been to teach my remaining son, Jeremy, who is fourteen years old, how to de-stress and cope with the many activities he is involved in. Hopefully that will make a difference for him. It's not until life is lost we think of how to save it, or how we might have been able to save it, as in my son, Clint's, case. I really listen to Jeremy and stop myself from pushing him too hard. He's a straight-A student, plays in the orchestra and is first string on the football team. We talk, that's our key to success. I listen. I have learned that children need to take time to 'smell the roses,' just as we do. They need to learn that it is important to take time just to regroup and recoup. That's not being lazy, it's being smart."

Stress can have a devastating impact on any of us. However, we wouldn't want to live without any stress at all. Some stress is desirable and even essential to life. Life would certainly be boring without stress; our time would be a humdrum, even-keeled, vanilla existence without change, excitement, love or challenge. Would any of us want to live like that?

Stress becomes a problem when it is not managed properly. Whether stress is caused by a major life change or by the cumulative effect of minor, everyday worries doesn't matter; how a child reacts to it can determine whether the stress is constructive or destructive.

Jim was a nine-year-old boy with "asthma" whose symptoms usually occurred *before* he played in his soccer games. Every Saturday morning during soccer season, as his family drove to the playing field, Jim said he would begin to feel "like there was an elephant" sitting on his chest. Then the wheezing would start.

Jim liked playing soccer, but he wasn't very good at it. His father spent countless hours practicing with him, making him kick the ball until it became so dark that they couldn't see anymore. Jim enjoyed spending time with his father, and he wanted to do well in his soccer games and make his dad proud.

The pressure was too much. Inhaled medications controlled Jim's wheezing, but he was too nervous to perform well on the soccer field. After each game, his father would encourage him and try to boost his son's spirits. However, Jim felt that he had disappointed his father . . . and he dreaded the prospect of doing it again the next week.

"Sometimes, the worst part about a stressful experience is anticipating it," says Dr. Bettie B. Youngs.[1] Jim was so stressed out about playing soccer that he developed pregame asthma. Other kids have headaches, nausea and vomiting, diarrhea, palpitations, and many other symptoms of stress.

No, we can't protect our children from all the stress they will encounter in their lives. We can, however, help prepare them for it and teach them how to deal with it so that it will not overwhelm them, make them sick and burn them out. Dr. Youngs calls this "psychological immunization": If we teach our children how to deal effectively with the smaller, more manageable stresses encountered every day, they will become psychologically more capable of dealing with the larger stressors in life.

Stress Management Techniques

Many ways are available to help your child deal with stress. What follows are some practical techniques we can use to make life in the pressure cooker more bearable. Many of these interventions are simple and based on common sense, yet we often neglect to do them. Others are more complicated and may require professional assistance. No magic bullet exists. What works for your child may not work for your neighbor's, which is why knowing your child is so important. You are in the best position to help him make the changes necessary to manage his stress. Psychologists, pediatricians and counselors can help you along the way, but your child's care is ultimately your responsibility.

Remember: if stress overwhelms us as parents, our children will probably find it harder to deal with their own stress. If we want them to heal, we should also work on healing ourselves.

Get Them to Express Themselves

Children often do not possess the self-awareness necessary to realize that they are feeling stress. Many adults don't either. Stress is intangible; you can't touch, taste, hear or smell it. Sometimes, though, just talking about stress can make a child feel better.

If you want to talk to your child about stress, you have to begin by listening. Don't just listen to their words, listen for the messages between the words. Be prepared for anything, and don't prejudge what they're telling you.

However, a child may not come to you and tell you, "I'm feeling a lot of stress because the 'cool kids' are ignoring me," or, "I'm stressed because, no matter how much I practice, I'll never be a very good soccer player. I know I'm going to let you down." You may have to encourage him to express his feelings. One way to do that is to share some of your own experiences with stress. Describe episodes when you were frustrated, when things didn't go the way you planned, when you were nervous, etc. If you think something specific is stressing your child, tell him about a similar experience that you had, especially one that you dealt with successfully.

I did that with my son, Jacob. He is a typical first-born child: competitive, driven, always wanting to be the best. He often puts a lot of pressure on himself to be perfect, and as a consequence, he gets stressed out even as my wife and I do our best to protect him from himself.

This desire became a problem during his first Little League game. We didn't realize it, but Jacob was nervous about playing in a real game with a lot of parents watching on the sidelines. Before the game started, he began to complain that he had a headache and didn't feel well. He gamely went out onto the field and played for two innings, but then said his head hurt too bad to play. He spent the rest of the game on the sidelines with his head in my wife's lap. On the ride home, Jacob vomited all over the interior of the car. At that, we chalked his symptoms up to illness.

The following week, Jacob again developed a headache just before the game started. This time he continued to play. He didn't vomit, but he continued to complain of a headache until after the game. We then put two and two together: Jacob, the perfectionist, was stressed out about making a mistake in front of everyone watching the game. We did all the right things: talked to him about relaxing on the field, told him we loved him whether he hit the ball well or not, explained that baseball is hard when you're only six years old, etc. Nothing seemed to make him feel better.

Then I shared my own experiences with performance anxiety. As a television reporter, I'm on the air live almost every day of the week, which provides a lot of opportunity to screw up in front of hundreds of thousands, and sometimes millions, of people.

And, believe me, I've made my share of mistakes during live performances. I told Jacob that when I first went from being a practicing physician to a television reporter, I would get so nervous before the red light on the camera went on that I, too, developed headaches. Only when I saw other reporters and anchors make mistakes and keep going did I stop expecting myself to be perfect each time I went on the air. That's when my performance-related headaches stopped.

When I told Jacob my own story, I saw his eyes open wide. He couldn't believe that I could ever have been nervous about being on television. He told me he felt the same way about Little League. But he also said that if I could screw up in front of all those viewers and joke about it, then he shouldn't worry if he didn't get a home run in every at bat. He hasn't had a baseball-related headache since!

If a child can't, or won't, talk about her stresses or concerns, you can use art as a way to help them vent. Preschoolers who can hold a crayon can use colors on paper to express their feelings.

One expert says:

"The artwork of an angry child will present quite a contrast to that of a child who is feeling content. Use the artwork as a media to help young children learn to label, understand and talk about their emotions. Place a variety of colored sheets done by children on the refrigerator or a wall and ask them what feeling each sheet has.

". . . Create every opportunity that can possibly be woven into life's scheme. Have body outlines available for children to color regarding their internal experiences. . . . The body outlines become a self-made mirror for the children, and provide adults with a means of helping the children to help themselves."[2]

Role-playing is another option. You can even use nonverbal role-playing for very young children. This technique can help children exaggerate a situation with their bodies and help you understand their emotions and frustrations.

Children who are old enough to write may find picking up a pen an effective way to unburden themselves. Former tennis star Guillermo Vilas once said, "When my life is going well, I live it. When it's not going well, I write it." Psychologist David Posen suggests that when his patients are angry, they "write a letter to the person at whom they are vexed. These letters are not for sending; they should be destroyed, unread, once they are written. The value is in expressing the feelings and getting them out. Rereading the letter just reinforces the upset and fans the flames of anger all over again."[3]

The important point is that everyone needs to be able to vent their worries, concerns, frustrations and anger. If not, stress can build up and cause the physical and psychological destruction we've seen throughout this book. We have to help our children find healthy, controlled ways in which they can vent their frustrations . . . and then move on with their lives. That task is not as easy as it sounds, but listening, talking and sharing are good ways to start.

Exercise

A good workout is about the best way to help melt your stress away. The same goes for our kids; when they are stressed, nervous energy builds up in their bodies. Exercise helps dissipate this pent-up energy.

Aerobic exercise has the best therapeutic effect. Luckily, when we let our children play—running, chasing, climbing, riding, rolling, etc.—they usually get the aerobic exercise they need to let off steam, as well as to keep their bodies and minds healthy.

The problem is that we are raising a generation of couch potatoes. Overall, one out of every five children in the United States is overweight. A child is often defined as obese if he weighs more than 20 percent more than he's supposed to for his height, or if he is higher than the eighty-fifth percentile for Body Mass Index (which is calculated by dividing the child's weight in kilograms by his height in meters squared).

By these definitions, approximately 13 percent of children (age six to eleven) and 14 percent of adolescents (age twelve to nineteen) are considered overweight, double the rate of thirty years ago.[4] Not surprisingly, researchers report that adolescents who sit and play video games instead of riding their bikes are more likely to put on excess weight and keep it on.

Although I know of no studies to prove a link between increasing rates of obesity and stress-induced illnesses in kids, I have a hunch that this dual increase is no coincidence. Certainly, obesity is related to plenty of other illness. Besides, exercise is good for people's mental health, no matter how old they are. On more than one occasion, I saw a child's chronic, severe, stress-induced headaches improve once he or she started a regular exercise regimen. In particular, I remember one twelve-year-old named John who had severe tension headaches for four years. John had seen many doctors and had been started on medications including antihistamines, antibiotics, painkillers and antidepressants. None of these medicines worked. When I saw John for the first time, I noticed that he was mildly overweight. As part of taking a good, thorough history, I asked him what kind of activities he liked. His only answers were "Playing Pokémon, playing Gameboy and watching TV." He did virtually no exercise at all. So, one of the first things I did was to start him on a program of regular exercise (in consultation with his pediatrician). Within two months, John's headaches had decreased by about 50 percent. They weren't cured, but they were markedly improved without using any medication.

Exercise causes nerves to release natural painkilling substances, called endorphins, into the body. However, endorphins do more than just relieve pain; they can elevate a person's mood. Endorphins are what make us feel great after a vigorous workout, the so-called runner's high. They also reduce the levels of the stress hormone, cortisol, in our bloodstreams. One recent study has even shown that intense physical activity may be the most effective way to reduce feelings of depression, anger and fatigue.[5]

The American Heart Association recommends children five and older participate in at least thirty minutes of enjoyable, moderate-intensity activities every day.[6] The AHA also recommends children perform at least thirty minutes of vigorous physical activities at least three to four days each week; they don't watch television or videotapes more than two hours a day (the rule in my house, in general, is one hour a day); school or day-care physical education include at least twenty minutes of coordinated large-muscle exercise; community recreational centers and schools offer a range of extracurricular programs to meet the needs and interests of specific populations, such as racial and ethnic minority groups, females, persons with disabilities, and low-income groups; and regular family outings that involve walking, cycling, swimming or other recreational activities.

Unfortunately, most of us don't follow those exercise recommendations. More than half of us don't get enough exercise, and about a quarter don't do any at all. However, we shouldn't let our children fall into the same rut. We don't have to hire personal trainers to make sure they exercise enough. All we have to do is give them a chance to do what kids do naturally, like play, run and sweat. We need to get them off the couch and onto the court, out of the backseat and into the backyard.

Breathing

Unless you have a problem with your lungs, you probably take breathing for granted. We do it subconsciously, that slow, rhythmic cycle of inspiration and expiration that doesn't stop until we die. Each breath of air brings oxygen into our bloodstream and releases the waste product, carbon dioxide. Breathing improperly can throw off our body's balance, making it more difficult for us to deal with stressful situations. Some evidence also shows that improper breathing, either too much or too little, can contribute to anxiety, panic attacks, depression, headaches and fatigue.

Conversely, there is medical evidence that deep breathing can help to relieve some of these stress-related conditions. Dr. Dean Ornish, author of *Dr.*

Dean Ornish's Program for Reducing Heart Disease: The Only System Scientifically Proven to Reverse Heart Disease Without Surgery or Drugs, says that the breath is the bridge between your mind and body. When your body feels stress, your breathing tends to become more rapid and shallow, your heart beats faster, and your muscles tense. Deep breathing stimulates your body to relax and reverses the physical changes brought on by stress. The heart slows, muscles relax, you feel better.

The Chinese have used deep breathing for centuries to decrease stress and promote physical and mental health. Qigong is an ancient Chinese art of meditation that consists mainly of deep, controlled breathing techniques, as well as physical exercise and massage techniques. "Qi" means breathing, and "gong" means work. Put the two together and you have a word meaning "breathing exercise." Practitioners say that Qigong promotes internal energy, healing, stress reduction and extended longevity.

Whatever you call it, deep breathing works in both adults and children. Children may find it especially helpful because they can do it without adult supervision whenever they feel stressed out. Children as young as five or six may even be able to do it.

Try this exercise with your child.

- Have him close his eyes and put his right hand on his abdomen, right at the waistline, and his left hand on his chest, right in the center. Ask him which hand rises as he takes a deep breath. Most of us under stress use our lung muscles instead of our abdominal diaphragm. However, slow, rhythmic, abdominal breathing helps us relax. We do it naturally when we sleep. That is why our voice is often deeper first thing in the morning. As the stress of the day increases, the muscles in our chest, neck and throat tend to tense, raising the pitch of our voice.

- With your child lying on his back, have him concentrate on slowly making his abdomen rise, instead of his chest, with each breath.
- When your child has mastered abdominal breathing, have him take long, slow, deep breaths through his nose. After he breathes in through his nose, have him pause, then slowly exhale, counting to himself, "One, two, three, four." The time it takes to breathe out should be about twice as long as the time it takes to breathe in. If your child follows this pattern, his breathing should begin to slow, and he should start to feel more relaxed.

If your child is stressed out, you may want to have him practice these deep-breathing exercises once or twice a day, for five to ten minutes each session. Mornings and evenings are probably the best times; that way, a child can take a few moments to relax before starting the day and another few moments at the end of the day to help him de-stress. In addition, he can resort to deep breathing any time he feels that stress is about to overwhelm him (a person does not have to be lying down to do deep-breathing exercises).

Visualization

John, an eight-year-old boy who attends a private school in the South, is a perfectionist. He comes from a middle-class family. His parents have repeatedly told him that they have "made many sacrifices so that [he] can get out of this life and move up in the world." He knows that his parents skimped and saved in order to pay for his private school education, and he feels a lot of pressure to get straight As in order to validate their sacrifices.

The burden of shouldering his parents' aspirations eventually caught up with him. John developed chronic intestinal problems, pain, diarrhea and cramps. His pediatrician could not determine the cause of the symptoms. However, the school counselor correctly surmised that John's problems were related to pressure. The counselor taught John to manage his stress with visualization therapy.

Visualization therapy is perhaps the best example of the power of the mind/body connection. We have seen throughout this book that when our mind is subjected to chronic stress, our body can manifest any number of symptoms. Visualization therapy turns this relationship on its head, using the mind to prevent physical symptoms. Some people even use visualization to help fight cancer. They use their imagination to visualize the immune cells in their body attacking invading cancer cells.

Visualization is a powerful stress management tool, especially for young children. Kids have very active imaginations, which we can use to guide them into a state of relaxation. In John's case, he was taught to close his eyes and imagine himself flying through the air, feeling light and uninhibited, swooping down to the school playground, then rising again high enough to brush against the clouds. Sometimes John imagines flying over his neighborhood; other times he flies over a favorite park. As he "flies," his mind and body relax. His stress fades into the background. After his visualization, he says he is better able to deal with situations or circumstances that would normally give him stomach pains.

How does visualization work? First, you ask your child to picture a place where he feels happy and comfortable. Second, have him close his eyes and take three deep breaths. Then, you guide him to the place he is visualizing. Here is an example of a visualization session taken from one I've used with Jacob when he suffers from one of his stress-related headaches (this technique is best done in a quiet room with the lights dimmed).

"What's your favorite thing to do, Jacob?" I ask.

"I like to bike ride," he answers.

"Okay, let's bike ride. Climb onto the bike. Do you feel the seat under your tush? (Pause for answer) Do you feel the handlebars in your hands? (Pause for answer) Start pumping your feet. (Pause) Feel your feet go up and down, up and down, up and down. (Pause) Feel the ground go under your wheels. Feel the wind in your hair. Ride up the street. Do you see that squirrel? (Pause for answer) Where do you want to go? (Answer) Oh, there's your friend Matthew. Say 'Hi' to Matthew. (Pause for him to say, 'Hi') Keep pedaling. Take a deep breath. Feel the air through your nose, fill up your chest and then rush out of your mouth. Pedal faster, up and down, up and down, up and down. See the ground whiz by? (Pause for answer) Take a few more deep breaths. (Pause) Feel the air going in and out, your feet pumping up and down. Okay, let's turn around and go home. Let the bike glide down the hill. Relax, relax your legs. Go slowly down the driveway until you come to a stop. Feel your feet touch the ground. The pavement is under your feet. Get off the bike. (Pause) Take three deep breaths, in and out, in and out, in and out. Get a nice cold glass of water. You're so thirsty. Feel how the water slides down your throat? Feels good, doesn't it? (Pause) Okay, it's time to relax now for a few minutes."

After that, I usually have Jacob breathe deeply a few more times and then leave him to relax for about ten minutes. When I go back into the room to get him, his stress has melted away.

Visualization can work in children of all ages. Of course, the place the children like to go or the things they like to do will differ depending on their maturity level and interests. The most important thing is to find a vision that the child feels comforting.

In many cases, like John's, children can learn to do visualization on their own whenever they encounter a stressful situation. Jacob is still young enough that he needs parental guidance to relax through visualization. However, in the next couple of years he should be able to do it on his own whenever he feels stressed or has a severe headache.

Meditation/Relaxation

A local gym in my town offers a yoga class for children, ages four to ten, every Sunday morning. When I first heard this, I laughed. Yoga for kids? I figured it was just a way for parents to get inexpensive babysitting while they exercised. While that may be true for some parents, others truly want their children to learn yoga in order to control their stress. Good for them! They are on the right track. In reality, though, how or why the children go there doesn't matter; the important thing is that they will have the chance to learn yoga.

Yoga is only one of many techniques a person can use to relax and de-stress. Visualization therapy, is another, as are meditation and hypnosis. The goal of each of these practices is to dissipate the toxic mental and physical stress energy that builds up in our bodies. And research shows that this can work. In one well-known study, people who practiced transcendental meditation had a lower heart rate; breathed more slowly; required less oxygen; had lower levels of the stress chemical, lactate, in their bloodstream; had a fourfold increase in skin resistance to electrical current, a sign of relaxation; and had increased brain alpha waves on their EEGs, also a sign of relaxation.

Harvard researcher Dr. Herbert Benson says that the body has an innate ability to enter into a special state of relaxation, which is characterized by lowered heart rate, slower breathing, lowered blood pressure, slower brain waves and reduced metabolism. He coined the term "relaxation response" in his landmark book of the same name.[7]

Dr. Benson says the physiological changes produced by the relaxation response counteract the harmful effects of stress. He describes the practice of the relaxation response technique.

1. Sit quietly in a comfortable position.
2. Close your eyes.
3. Deeply relax all your muscles, beginning at

your feet and progressing up to your face. Keep them relaxed.

4. Breathe through your nose. Become aware of your breathing. As you breathe out, say the word, "One," silently to yourself. Breathe easily and naturally.

5. Continue for ten to twenty minutes. You may open your eyes to check the time, but do not use an alarm. When you finish, sit quietly for several minutes, at first with your eyes closed and later with your eyes opened. Do not stand for a few minutes.

6. Maintain a passive attitude and permit relaxation to occur at its own pace. When distracting thoughts occur, try to ignore them by not dwelling on them and return to repeating, "One." With practice, the response should come with little effort. Practice the technique once or twice daily, but not within two hours after any meal, since the digestive processes seem to interfere with the elicitation of the relaxation response.[8]

Children may find Dr. Benson's relaxation response technique difficult, especially if they are young. However, achieving the relaxation response doesn't have to be so complicated. Your child can accomplish it by just sitting quietly in the backyard, lying on a bed, petting an animal or doing any other activity in which she is resting peacefully.

One school-based study, involving school nurses administering relaxation training to children for five to six weeks, showed relaxation therapy to be "a practical and possibly also cost-effective intervention for children with recurrent tension headaches."

The researchers suggested that relaxation training should probably be the primary treatment for kids with chronic tension headaches.[9]

Teach your child to isolate different body parts and relax them with each slow breath she exhales. For example, while lying on the floor, instruct her to tighten or squeeze her toes on the left foot, then relax with a deep breath. Now tighten her left knee and upper leg . . . then relax and breathe. Proceed in this fashion to the right side of the lower body, to the abdomen and upper body, each arm, hand and fingers, chest, neck, jaws, and face.

How well does meditation work? In one study, researchers found that medical students had higher blood levels of stress hormones during stressful test periods than they did during nonstress times, but the researchers also wanted to see if they could use stress management techniques to reduce the students' stress hormone levels.

The researchers taught half of the medical students hypnosis and relaxation training prior to taking their exams. During the exams, they compared the immune function of students in the training group with that of the students who received no relaxation training. "We saw no difference at first," says Dr. Janice Kiecolt-Glaser, the psychologist who conducted the study. "Students in the relaxation group showed the same average downward alterations in immune function as the others. But a closer look showed that the students trained in relaxation varied tremendously in how often they practiced their relaxation techniques. And those who took their relaxation seriously, who practiced the techniques often, showed significantly better immune function during exams than did those who practiced less frequently or not at all."[10]

Biofeedback

Most of our body's stress response occurs automatically. We don't think about breathing faster, tensing our muscles, grinding our teeth, etc. Our body is preprogrammed to act that way when subjected to chronic stress. Biofeedback uses instruments to make us aware of these automatic functions of our body. Once we can detect these automatic physical responses, biofeedback can help us control them and potentially reverse the stress response.

Biofeedback is especially effective in children, perhaps because they like the computer games and gadgets involved, or maybe because children do not have the burden of having spent thirty, forty, fifty or more years ignoring their stress responses, as many of us have.

Biofeedback teaches a child what it feels like to relax. A biofeedback machine can detect indications of stress, such as muscle tension, pulse rate, and changes in the skin and body temperature. The machine converts those readings into signals the child can understand, such as a repeating sound or a bouncing ball on a computer screen. The child is then taught a relaxation technique. As he begins to relax, he can see it on the computer screen. The more he relaxes, the more the figure on the screen changes. In time, he tunes in to his body and learns to control it without using the biofeedback machine. If successful, the child will be able to lower his muscle tension, decrease his heart rate and lower his blood pressure when he's confronted with a stressful situation.

One physician recently told me about a seventeen-year-old girl who had been completely healthy until she left for college. As a freshman, she developed incapacitating migraines every time she had to take a test. By the end of the year, it was clear that the migraines were interfering with her grades. The final straw came when she was unable to take her final exam for her English class because she had severe head pain, nausea and vomiting. When she returned home on a school break, her mom wisely took her to a psychologist to learn biofeedback. So far, the physician says, the biofeedback is working. The girl still feels stress about her tests, but she's now able to prevent the physical stress response, her migraine headaches, from occurring. Instead of missing tests, she's now acing them.

That girl's experience is not unique, and it applies to younger children, too. Even children as young as four years old can benefit from this form of therapy. A preliminary study in Amsterdam found that three children, ages four, five and six, who suffered from frequent, severe migraines, had a significant improvement in their symptoms after learning biofeedback in combination with relaxation and pain-coping techniques. Two of the children became headache-free with behavioral treatment, while the other showed a 60 percent decrease in headaches.[11]

Many companies make small, personal biofeedback monitors that can be used at home. I know a lot of patients with chronic headaches who have improved by using these devices in combination with a relaxation tape. However, in my experience, children should begin their biofeedback training with a trained professional, often a psychologist. Once a child becomes proficient with biofeedback, then trying it on his own is more reasonable.

General Tips

We can help our children deal with stress in other ways, too. We can help them prioritize when they feel overwhelmed by responsibilities and activities. Which ones are most important? Which are the most immediate? Which are the most enjoyable? Often a child is not mature enough to take a step back and ask those crucial questions. However, we can help him do so and hopefully provide some stress relief at the same time.

We also need to make sure our children eat right and get enough sleep. Food is the energy that allows the body to function. Without the proper balance of vitamins, minerals and nutrients, the body won't function properly. You wouldn't think of mixing sand with gasoline when you fill your car's tank; the engine would quickly grind to a halt. Yet many of us do something similar when we fill our children full of junk food. More than half of the food our children eat is processed. Much of the rest is filled with additives and preservatives. Children have become addicted to soda, candy and other junk food.

What we eat affects how we function, both physically and emotionally. Our children deal with stress best when their bodies and minds operate at peak efficiency. When they eat an unbalanced, junk-heavy diet, they will be more susceptible to the ravaging effects of stress. We cannot completely control what our children put into their mouths. But we can do our part by providing them with "three squares" a day. You may even want to consult a dietitian if your child suffers symptoms of chronic stress. A balanced diet won't make stress disappear but may help protect against the consequences of stress.

The same goes for sleep. Fatigue depletes our body and mind of the energy needed to fight the effects of stress. Experts say that "when distressed people get more sleep, they feel better and are more resilient and adaptable in dealing with day-to-day events."[12] We do have some control over how much our children sleep. If they are constantly tired, worn down or frequently sick, you should probably keep track of how much (or, more precisely, how little) they sleep. You can't make them sleep, but you can set up the proper conditions to allow them to get enough rest. You can take a number of steps to put your child on a normal sleep cycle.

- Have him go to bed earlier
- Make sure his room is dark and quiet when he goes to bed
- Limit the time he spends on the computer or telephone at night
- Don't let him watch TV in bed
- Cut caffeine out of his diet, especially at night
- Wake him up at a consistent time each morning
- When he wakes up, open the shades and let the sunlight in. Bright light helps to reset the body's sleep cycle.

Sleep, nutrition, relaxation, meditation, biofeedback, counseling, drawing, role-playing, visualization, breathing, exercise, discussion . . . almost as many ways are available to deal with stress as there are stressed-out people. No technique is 100 percent successful or appropriate for every child, and many of these techniques complement each other. For example, eating right and getting enough sleep will help a child who is trying to learn biofeedback. You and your child have to figure out which techniques will best help him deal with life in the pressure cooker. If one doesn't work, try another. Dealing with stress is difficult under the best of circumstances, but it's worth the effort. What we do now can prepare our children to deal with life's unavoidable stresses in a healthy, practical way. That legacy is one of the best we can bequeath them.

ELEVEN

CELEBRATING YOUR CHILD

It's the Little Things. . . .

We are largely responsible for the formation of our children's self-image. Our words, actions, facial expressions and gestures send messages to our children. If we send positive signals, our children will likely feel good about themselves. If we send negative messages, we can destroy our children's sense of self-worth. These subconscious impressions often determine the way a child sees himself for the rest of his life. Children need nature and nurture to succeed.

"Accentuating the positive is more a *way of life* than a parenting technique," writes Katrina Katarelis, a mother of two children. "It involves taking the time to recognize and acknowledge the ordinary *and* extraordinary things children do every day. It takes a bit of our time and attention to 'catch them being good,' but with practice it gets much easier. By accentuating the positive, children begin to feel cherished simply because of who they are, not what they do."[1]

Cyndi, a work-at-home mother of two girls, says she works hard to accentuate the positive by feeling good about her children's small accomplishments as well as their larger ones. She says that one way she does this is by teaching her kids to be ". . . relaxed about living. In the summer, we run in the sprinklers, play in the pool, water plants, collect bugs and play in the dirt.

"My five-year-old can tell you about all the fruit trees that we have growing and the roses and the difference between lilacs and lavender. They are healthy, happy, vibrant and vital. They are wonderful, and I wouldn't change a thing."

Many of us have trouble being "relaxed about living." I know I do. I'm goal-oriented, competitive, driven, ambitious and totally stressed out. I enjoy my three children, and I try to spend as much time with them as I possibly can. But I sometimes find that I turn what should be a fun activity into just another lesson or task designed to make my children "better." I have to remind myself that when my son wants to go out in the backyard and play catch, he just wants to have fun horsing around with me, even if he can't catch the ball very well. He doesn't want me to correct his catching or throwing technique each time we toss the ball. That activity is not fun, but rather it is work for both of us.

What is more important, spending time playing catch with my son or making sure he doesn't let a ground ball go through his legs? The answer, of course, is that the mere act of spending time with my child will do more for his emotional development than whether he makes the high school baseball team. The joy of being together should be therapeutic for both of us.

Ask yourself this question: How many activities or conversations with your parents do you remember from your childhood? A few of them probably stand out in your mind. In general, though, you probably don't recall most of the interactions you had with your parents. On the other hand, each of you can probably describe the intangible aspects of your relationship with your parents, how they treated you, how they reacted in the face of a problem and how often they were there for you.

Every interaction we have with our children forms an impression in their subconscious minds. When we laugh with them, they feel our joy. When we forget about our own problems and spend time with them, they feel important. When we indicate that we're disappointed in them, they feel like failures.

We tend to be good at accentuating the positive for the big things like grades, sports and recitals. Everyday "triumphs" sometimes get lost in the mix. However, the little things matter most, like coloring pictures, performing a show in the living room, kicking a soccer ball, getting dressed by themselves, saying "please" and "thank you." Accentuating the positive about a child's actions, no matter how small or inconsequential, stamps his brain with subconscious messages like "I'm good," or "I'm worthwhile," or "I'm important." We remember those things when we grow up. They shape us far more than whether we learn to read at age four or at age six.

"The joy a child experiences works much like an emotional vaccine," says one family therapist. "It's something that will protect us later, when we're adults and life throws us the inevitable curve."[2] Finding joy in our children's small accomplishments and letting them see our joy is what celebrating our children is all about.

Celebrating your child can take many different

forms. The easiest, and perhaps most important, thing you can do is show interest in what they're doing. Too often we hear them without really listening. Many of us are so good at multitasking that we neglect to focus our full attention on what our children say or do. Paying attention to a person is a powerful statement in itself. When you do that, you tell the other person in no uncertain terms that they are important.

If you doubt the power of paying attention, just talk to anyone who has met President Bill Clinton. Almost everyone who has done so will tell you that when he talks to you, he focuses his attention on you like a laser beam. You feel as though, at that moment, you are the most interesting and important person in the world. Afterward he may not even remember that he met you, but you come away from the encounter with a positive, warm feeling. Whatever you think of him, his ability to pay attention contributes mightily to his charismatic reputation.

When our children were old enough to talk, my wife and I started a tradition that we hoped would let our children know we were paying attention to them and that we cared about what went on in their lives. We call it "best/worst." Every night during dinner (or during "fruit chat" when my wife or I don't get home early enough from work to have dinner with the kids), we go around the table, one by one, and talk about the best and worst parts of our day. On most nights, the answers are mundane: "My best was that I got to play with Allie (my daughter's best friend) after school today." Or, "My worst is that I fell down during gym and scraped my knee." On other nights, the kids have more important issues to discuss. But no matter what, we listen and talk about everyone's day as if it was the most important thing in the world. Our kids love it; they always call out, "I'm first at best/worst," as soon as dinner (or fruit chat) starts. Another benefit of "best/worst" is that my wife and I have a chance to detect any potential problems in our kids' lives before they turn into major issues.

Praise and encouragement are also important in building a child's self-esteem. Dr. Sal Severe says that a little praise can go a long way: "Success creates internal motivation. When your boss praises your work, you feel successful and continue to work hard. You can use success to give your *child* a boost of internal motivation. Point out your child's good behavior and decisions. Your child will feel successful. Success motivates him to work harder."[3]

Love, affection, encouragement and support are usually more effective than flash cards and mind-bending videotapes.

Hard work and success are only parts of the equation. Enjoying life is another. When you accentuate the positive, you can help your children achieve both. You may also find that focusing on your children's daily accomplishments helps you forget about your own worries, problems or issues. Thus, by taking steps to instill in your child a healthy self-esteem, you may inadvertently de-stress your own life and set a good example of how to live.

You *can* have your cake and eat it, too!

Fingerprints

"I probably pushed my oldest son into baseball and soccer a little too hard," says Wayne, a father of two active boys, "although now he has been playing baseball for seven straight seasons and soccer for four straight seasons. The two sports complement each other well, and baseball is still his favorite sport. I tried pushing my younger son, and he did one year of baseball and one year of soccer and that's it. I am going to just let him be his own person as he is very artistic, and a friend even suggested karate for him."

Two sons. Same parents. Totally different interests. Sound familiar? Children are like fingerprints, no two are alike. Even identical twins often have very different likes, dislikes, wants, needs, hopes, desires, passions, skills and abilities.

A school counselor in New York City once said to me, "Everyone at this school comes here and has a talent. Every kid has a talent. If you overstress them or put too much pressure and don't give time for their talent to unfold, it will stymie them." Too often, we don't appreciate our children's special talents. In part, we're too busy working, carpooling or dealing with our own issues. But we may also fail to appreciate our children's talents because they are not the same as ours. They do not conform to the ideal of what we want from a child.

It reminds me of an old joke: The mother of the president is at the inauguration and the secretary of state is sitting next to her. The secretary of state turns to her and says, "You must be very proud of your son." She nods and replies, "Yeah, he has a great medical practice. And this one did all right, too." Sometimes, we make our children feel like nothing they do is good enough to please us.

Psychologist Donald Cohen, in a series of letters to his father, discussed how as a child he had difficulty trying to match up to his father's expectations: "You wanted me to be you, I wanted you to be me. . . . I felt that you wanted me to be someone important, to make something of myself. Those expectations intimidated me and seemed to contribute to my fear of competition and success. There was encouragement at times to be my own person, but sometimes I felt that you had an agenda for who I should be. This would often get in the way of my being able to pursue my own dreams."[4]

On average, our children contain 50 percent of our genes. However, their personalities and talents may still be 100 percent different than ours. One of the keys to raising a happy, healthy child is to find his or her particular talents and desires, nurture them and provide encouragement. In many cases, nature will do the rest.

One mom told me, "I was a dancer growing up and I always wanted my daughter to follow in my footsteps. From the day she was born, I hung posters of dancers in her room, showed her dancing videos and bought every toy I could find that was in any way related to dancing. When she was old enough, I enrolled her in dance classes and encouraged her as much as possible.

"There was only one thing I forgot to do—ask *her* if *she* wanted to dance. Turns out that she had no interest in it. She was happier playing baseball with her boy friends or just making mud pies in the backyard."

The girl had stomachaches every time she went to dance class. Her mom thought it was a case of nerves, when it was really a manifestation of stress from being forced to fulfill her mother's dreams. When her mother realized this, she had trouble coming to terms with the fact that her daughter didn't share her ambitions. It was also difficult to accept her daughter's "tomboyish" behavior. Eventually, however, she began to accept her daughter for who she was. She reveled in her daughter's ability to "keep up with the boys" and praised the girl when she brought home "cake and cookies" make out of pebbles and mud. The girl's stomachaches stopped, and her mom felt less stressed about creating the next Debbie Allen.

A school guidance counselor told me a similar story: Jill had always dreamed of playing the piano but never had the opportunity to learn while she was growing up. Now that she was an adult, Jill transferred her desires onto her daughter, signing the child up for private piano lessons. There was only one problem: her daughter had no interest in playing the piano. She threw a fit every time she had a lesson. Jill was distraught. Eventually, she approached the guidance counselor for help. The counselor came up with a very practical solution: instead of forcing her daughter to play the piano, Jill would fulfill her dream by taking lessons herself. A few months later, Jill was playing "Chopsticks" on the keyboard and letting her daughter play the games *she* chose to play. Both were happy as they busily pursued their own interests.

Gold Medals

A couple of years ago, I had the honor of presenting awards at the Connecticut Special Olympics games. The children gathered from all over the state, some were in wheelchairs, some limped, some used crutches, others were mentally disabled. What they all had in common was their enthusiasm for the games, their sheer joy at just being able to participate in a sport. When each of these kids crossed the finish line, big smiles broke out across their faces, and they usually gave a big hug to whoever happened to be closest to them. Whether they finished first or last didn't matter. They were all winners and the Special Olympics staff treated every participant that way.

I often think about those children. Each of them was disabled in one way or another. That didn't matter to the parents, friends, officials and spectators at the games. They celebrated these children for their effort and unique abilities. If only we could learn to treat our own children with the same degree of arms-wide-open acceptance, we would likely see more of them smiling instead of being stressed out.

We live in a competitive world, full of people with scowling, frowning faces who only judge themselves relative to those around them. To these people, life is like one giant Olympics. Competition is all that matters. They consider anything less than first place a failure.

Yet, these win-at-all-cost people are often the ones failing at the most important thing they'll ever do in their lives: raising stable children. Their children are the ones who frequently end up in doctors' offices or on psychologists' couches. These parents often fail to recognize that life may be a rat race, but every child is making a way to his or her own finish line. Some are sprinters. Others are marathoners. Still others walk. The journey is what counts most. If a child crosses his own, unique finish line, he's a winner. Thus, every child can be a gold medalist in life, if we let him run *his* race, instead of expecting him to run ours.

NOTES

Chapter 1

[1] *www.pbs.org/wgbh/zoom.*
[2] Ibid.
[3] Michael Matza, "Israelis Provide Lesson in Coping with Terrorism: Intelligence Key to Thwarting Plans," *Philadelphia Inquirer,* 22 September 2001.
[4] Lisa Rabasca, "More Psychologists in the Trenches," *Monitor on Psychology* 31, no. 6 (June 2000).
[5] Debby Waddell and Alex Thomas, "Disaster: Helping Children Cope. A Handout for Parents," National Association of School Psychologists.
[6] *www.ncptsd.org.*
[7] *Journal of the American Academy of Child and Adolescent Psychiatry* 37, no. 10 (October 1998), supplement.
[8] Michael Hollander and Janna Hobbs, "Tips for Talking with the Kids in Your Lives," McLean Hospital, Belmont, Massachusetts.
[9] Patricia Sheets, press release from University of Alabama at Birmingham.

Chapter 2

[1] *Athens (Georgia) Daily News Online,* 3 May 1999.
[2] Bettie B. Youngs, *Stress and Your Child* (Fawcett Columbine, 1995).
[3] Margot Maine, Personal interview.
[4] News report, WVIT-TV, West Hartford, Conn., 19 February 2001.
[5] *www.beautyworlds.com/aboutbeauty.htm.*
[6] Paula Moynahan, Televised interview. WVIT–TV.
[7] *http://expage.com/iamanorexic.*
[8] David Elkind, *The Hurried Child* (New York: Perseus Books, 1988).
[9] "The Hurried Child Revisited," by Carleton Kendrick. The Learning Network, 2001 (Web site).
[10] American Academy of Pediatrics. Joint Statement on the Impact of Entertainment Violence on Children, Congressional Public Health Summit, July 26, 2000.
[11] *Healthscout.com.*

[12] Kaiser Family Foundation, "Talking with Kids about Tough Issues" survey.

[13] *www.kff.org.*

[14] *www.cnn.com.*

Chapter 3

[1] Ibid.

[2] Scot Meyer, "The Stress Syndrome," Healthscout.com, 8 May 2001.

[3] Joan Arehart-Treichel, "Stress More Toxic to Brain Than Researchers Thought," *Psychiatric News*, 19 May 2000.

[4] *Merriam Webster's Medical Dictionary*, 1995.

[5] Steven L. Burns, "The Medical Basis of Stress, Depression, Anxiety, Sleep Problems, and Drug Use," *www.teachhealth.com/#recogstress.*

[6] Matt Gorkin, as quoted on *stressdoc.com.*

[7] *Psychology Today*, January/February 1996.

[8] Arehart-Treichel, *"Stress More Toxic to Brain Than Researchers Thought."*

[9] *Journal of Psychosomatic Research* 43, no. 3 (September 1997): 271-78.

[10] *Psychosomatics* 34, no. 6 (November-December 1993): 485-93.

[11] *Journal of School Health* 61, no. 2 (February 1991): 86-91.

[12] *Pain* 77, no. 1 (July 1998): 67-72.

[13] *Jet*, 16 October 1995.

[14] *Lancet*, 10 August 1996.

[15] Esther Sternberg, *The Balance Within* (W.H. Freeman and Company, 2000).

[16] Jeffrey Kluger with Alice Park, "The Quest for a Super Kid," *Time*, 30 April 2001.

[17] David Elkind, *The Hurried Child* (New York: Perseus Books, 1988).

[18] Ibid.

[19] W. T. Boyce, S. Adams, J. M. Tschann, F. Cohen, D. Wara, and M. R. Gunnar, "Adrenocortical and Behavioral Predictors of Immune Responses to Starting School," *Pediatric Research* 38 (1995): 1009-17.

[20] W. T. Boyce, M. Chesney, A. Alkon-Leonard, J. M. Tschann, S. Adams, B. Chesterman, F. Cohen, P. Kaiser, S. Folkman, and D. Wara, "Psychobiologic Reactivity to Stress and Childhood Respiratory Illnesses: Results of Two Prospective Studies," *Psychosomatic Medicine* 57 (1995): 411-22.

[21] S. B. Manuck, S. Cohen, B. S. Rabin, M. F. Muldoon, E. A. Bachen, "Individual Differences in Cellular Immune Response to Stress," *Psychological Science* 2 (1991): 111-14.

[22] *Neuroscience Letter* 315, no. 1-2 (23 November 2001): 17-20.

[23] *Psychiatry Research* 104, no. 2 (2001): 109-17.

[24] That is, we need to recognize the extent of the mind-body connection.

Chapter 4

[1] Meyer Friedman and Ray H. Rosenman, Type A Behavior and Your Heart (New York: Fawcett Crest, 1974).

[2] Alvin Rosenfeld and Nicole Wise, *Hyper-Parenting: Are You Hurting Your Child by Trying Too Hard?* (St. Martin's Press, 2000).

[3] Telephone interview with Dr. John Friel.

[4] Dr. Tara Donnelly, as quoted in "How Stress Strikes," by Cindy Schweich Hundler, *Woman's Day*, Oct. 7, 1977.

[5] U.S. Trust Survey of Affluent Americans, 2000.

[6] Personal interview.

[7] Personal interview.

[8] Telephone interview.
[9] David Elkind, *The Hurried Child* (New York: Perseus Books, 1988).
[10] Telephone interview.
[11] Telephone interview.
[12] Television interview, CBC News, Aug. 27, 1999.
[13] Diana Bohmer, Mind/Body Medical Institute.
[14] R. Fornara, et al., "Family Therapy: The Focus on Headache as Conflictual Behaviour Epiphenomenon," *Cephalalgia Supplement* 16 (1995), 3rd Congress on Headache in Childhood and Adolescence.
[15] One-parent families are much more likely to end up on welfare than two-parent families.
[16] Personal e-mail.
[17] *cnn.com*, March 8, 2001.
[18] Kaiser Family Foundation, "Talking with Kids about Tough Issues."

Chapter 5
[1] Telephone interview.
[2] Bettie B. Youngs, *Stress and Your Child* (New York: Fawcett Columbine, 1995).
[3] Beth Levine, "Is Your Child Too Stressed?" *Redbook,* December 1995.
[4] op cit.

Chapter 6
[1] Sandra Hofferth, "Healthy Environments, Healthy Children: Children in Families," A Report on the 1997 Panel Study of Income Dynamics, University of Michigan, November 1998.
[2] *NY Journal News,* 13 April 2000.
[3] *NY Journal News,* 13 May 1999.
[4] David Ghitelman, "Kids on Overload: Is Your Child's Schedule Tighter Than Your Own?" *Spotlight,* January 2000.
[5] Cindy Schweich Handler, "The Importance of Doing Nothing," *Parenting,* May 1999.
[6] Helen Cordes, "Kids Who Do Too Much," *Child,* September 2000.
[7] "Busy Around the Clock," *Newsweek,* 17 July 2000.
[8] Cordes, "Kids Who Do Too Much."
[9] *Journal of Epidemiology and Community Health,* January 2002; 56:89–94.
[10] R. E. Anderson et al, "Relationship of Physical Activity and Television Watching with Body Weight and Levels of Fatness Among Children: Results from the Third National Health and Nutrition Examination Survey." *Journal of the American Medical Association,* 25 March 1998; 279 (12): 938–942.
[11] *www.aacap.org/web/aacap/publications/factsfam/tv.htm.*

Chapter 7
[1] *USA Weekend,* 24-26 December 1999.
[2] *Scholastic Parent & Child,* December/January 2001.
[3] *Envisagedesign.com.*
[4] Ibid.
[5] Josh Shonkoff, quoted in *U.S. News & World Report,* 13 September 1999.
[6] "Fertile Minds," *Time,* February 3, 1997.
[7] David Elkind, *Miseducation: Preschoolers At Risk* (Knopf, 1998).
[8] "Parents," November 1998.
[9] "Types of Sports Injuries and How They Can Be Prevented." Presentation

to "Safe State Injury Prevention in Massachusetts" program, September 18, 1996.

10 *The Physician and Sports Medicine*, 27, No. 1 (January 1999).
11 "NBC Nightly News," 14 February 2001.
12 Telephone interview.
13 Children's Television Workshop Website.
14 Telephone interview
15 Zero to Three Website: *www.zerotothree.org.*
16 *Newsweek,* Special Issue, fall/winter 2000.
17 Elkind, *Miseducation.*
18 *Newsweek,* Special Issue, fall/winter 2000.
19 *Scholastic Parent & Child,* December/January 2001.
20 *The Journal News* (New York), 16 March 2000.
21 Telephone interview.

Chapter 8

1 Kyodo News, 6 June 1998.
2 *New York Times,* 25 February 2001.
3 Ibid.
4 Survey conducted by Applied Research & Consulting for American Toy Institute, Inc., cited in KidSource Online, 26 August 1999.
5 Harvard College Admissions Office Website.
6 E-mail.
7 Digital High Website.
8 *The Times,* 27 May 1996.
9 *The Shambhala Dictionary of Taoism* (Shambhala Publications, 1996).
10 Andree Brooks, "Educating the Children of Fast-Track Parents," *Phi Delta Kappan* 71, no. 8 (April 1990): 612-15.
11 Newschannel 2000.com, 7 July 2000.
12 *Count on Shell* 1, no. 4 (summer 1999).
13 June Million, "Securing High-Stakes Tests from Cheating," *Education Digest,* November 2000.
14 "Ritalin's Routine Use Raises Alarm over Diagnoses Goals," *Detroit News,* 8 March 1998.
15 "The Merrow Report," *www.pbs.org.*
16 Matt Scherbel, "Ritalin Ain't the Answer," *The Pyle Print,* as quoted on *www.attentiondeficit.50megs.com/mattsstory.htm.*
17 *www.outlookcities.com/children/.*
18 Telephone interview.
19 Telephone interview.
20 Telephone interview.
21 Highwired.com, 14 April 2000.
22 Telephone interview.
23 Actually, Morpheus said, "I can show you the door; you're the one who has to walk through it." But Morpheus was only talking to a single person.
24 The *Journal News,* (New York) 13 April 2000.
25 Susan Black, "A Wake-Up Call on High School Starting Times," *Education Digest,* December 2000.
26 Kyla Wahlstrom, "Don't Start High School without the Kids!" *Education Digest,* September 2000.
27 *Chicago Tribune,* January 18, 1999.
28 Sandra Hofferth, "Healthy Environments, Healthy Children: Children in Families," 1997 Panel Study of Income Dynamics, Child Development Supplement, 1998.

[29] Harris Cooper et al, "Relationships Among Attitudes About Homework Assigned and Completed and Student Achievement," *Tennessee State University Journal of Educational Psychology.* Vol. 90. No. 1.

[30] "Homework Doesn't Help," *Newsweek,* March 1998.

[31] Christine Sandulli, "Under Pressure," *http://wellesleytownsman.com/specils/teens/story1.html.*

[32] *www.egroups.com/group/parentsunitedforsafehomework.*

[33] *www.courierpress.com.*

[34] Telephone interview.

[35] Telephone interview.

[36] Adapted from the Ann Landers column, 30 June 2000.

Chapter 9

[1] Vern Seefeldt et al, "Overview of Youth Sports Programs in the United States," Youth Sports Institute, Michigan State University. Commisioned by the Carnegie Council on Adolescent Development for Its Task Force on Youth Development and Community Programs.

[2] *Time,* July 12, 1999.

[3] Fred Engh, *Why Johnny Hates Sports* (Avery, 1999).

[4] Ibid.

[5] Study conducted by Northern Kentucky University, 1994. Reported to me by Greg Bach, Communications Director, National Alliance for Youth Sports.

[6] Associated Press Report. *Amarillo Globe-News,* July 13, 2000.

[7] Ibid.

[8] Published in *Medicine & Science in Sports & Exercise,* the journal of the American College of Sports Medicine.

[9] As quoted on Healthscout.com, 22 February 2000.

[10] U.S. Consumer Product Safety Commission report.

[11] *www.masc.state.mn.us/resources/index.html.*

[12] Fred Engh, *Why Johnny Hates Sports* (Avery, 1999).

[13] "We're All Number 1," *Time,* 22 June 1998.

[14] *Time,* August 14, 2000.

[15] Jim and Janet Sundberg, *How to Win at Sports Parenting* (Water Brook, 2000).

[16] Colonel Edwin E. "Buzz" Aldrin Jr., with Wayne Warga, *Return to Earth* (Random House, 1973).

Chapter 10

[1] Bettie B. Youngs, *Stress and Your Child* (New York: Fawcett Columbine, 1985).

[2] Janai Lowenstein, *Journal of Physical Education, Recreation and Dance.* (February 1991), *www.cliving.org/apple.htm.*

[3] David Posen, "Stress Management for the Patient and Physician," *The Canadian Journal of Continuing Medical Education* (April 1995), *www.mentalhealth.com/mag1/p51-str.html.*

[4] Liane M. Summerfield, "Promoting Physical Activity and Exercise among Children," *www.kidsource.com.*

[5] *www.drkoop.com/wellness/fitness/files/depression.asp.*

[6] American Heart Association, *www.justmove.org.*

[7] Herbert Benson, *The Relaxation Response* (New York: William Morrow and Company, 1977).

[8] *www.green-river.com/assign34.htm.*

[9] B. Larsson, and J. Calsson, "Psychological Treatment of Tension

Headaches in School Children," *Cephalalgia Supplement* 16 (1995), 3rd Congress on Headache in Childhood and Adolescence.

[10] *pni.psychiatry.ohio-state.edu/jkg/index.htm#Medical%20Student.*

[11] H. van tier Helm-Hylkema, "Effects of a Short Structured Behaviour Therapy on Migraine of Young Migraine Patients," *Cephalalgia Supplement* 16 (1995), 3rd Congress on Headache in Childhood and Adolescence.

[12] Posen, "Stress Management for the Patient and Physician," *www.mental-health.coj/mag1/p51-str.html.*

Chapter 11

[1] Katrina Katarelis, "A Recipe for Growing Happy Children," *Parent and Preschooler Newsletter,* December 1995.

[2] Joanne Kaufman, "Give Them Their Vitamins, Minerals and a Daily Dose of Joy," *Good Housekeeping,* November 2000.

[3] Sal Severe, *How to Behave, So Your Children Will, Too.* (Greentree Publishing, 1997).

[4] Max Cohen and Donald Cohen, *My Father, My Son* (Bethel, Conn.: Rutledge Books, 1996).

RECOMMENDED READING

The Hurried Child: Growing Up Too Fast Too Soon, by David Elkind, Ph.D. (Perseus Books, 1989).

The 7 Worst Things Good Parents Do, by John C. Friel, Ph.D., and Linda D. Friel, M.A. (HCI, 1999).

Hyper-Parenting: Are You Hurting Your Child by Trying Too Hard? by Alvin Rosenfeld, M.D., and Nicole Wise (St. Martin's Press, 2000).

How to Behave So Your Children Will, Too! by Sal Severe, Ph.D. (Viking, 2000).

The Myth of the First Three Years: A New Understanding of Early Brain Development and Lifelong Learning, by John T. Bruer, Ph.D. (Free Press, 1999).

The Scientist in the Crib: Minds, Brains, and How Children Learn, by Alison Gopnik, Ph.D., Andrew N. Meltzoff, Ph.D., and Patricia K. Kuhl, Ph.D. (Morrow, 1999).

The Balance Within: The Science Connecting Health and Emotions, by Esther M. Sternberg, M.D. (Freeman, 2000).

Stress and Your Child: Helping Kids Cope with the

Strains and Pressures of Life, by Bettie B. Youngs, Ph.D., Ed.D. (Fawcett Columbine, 1985).

Type A Behavior and Your Heart, by Meyer Friedman, M.D., and Ray H. Rosenman, M.D. (Fawcett Crest, 1974).

Miseducation: Preschoolers at Risk, by David Elkind, Ph.D. (Knopf, 1998).

The End of Homework: How Homework Disrupts Families, Overburdens Children, and Limits Learning, by Etta Kralovec, John Buell (Beacon Press, 2000).

The Battle Over Homework: Common Ground for Administrators, Teachers, and Parents, by Harris Cooper (Corwin, 2001).

How to Win at Sports Parenting: Maximizing the Sports Experience for You and Your Child, by Jim and Janet Sundberg (Waterbrook, 2000).

Why Johnny Hates Sports: Why Organized Youth Sports Are Failing Our Children and What We Can Do About It, by Fred Engh (Avery, 1999).

Tuesdays with Morrie: An Old Man, a Young Man, and Life's Greatest Lesson, by Mitch Albom (Doubleday, 1997).